My First Best Friend

My First Best Friend

Thirty Stories

*

Lifetime Memories

By Nancy Lindemeyer

Foreword by Denise Di Novi

Original Poems by Robin Reiser

Stewart, Tabori & Chang
NEW YORK

See, see my playmate,
Come out and play with me
And bring your dollies three.
Climb up my apple tree,
Holler down my rain barrel,
Slide down my cellar door,
And we'll be jolly friends
Forever evermore.

Philip Wingate, "Two Little Maids" (1894)

To Janice Foster Barth,

my very own first best friend,

and in memory of

Bertha Maude Keithley,

always

Contents

Foreword

My lifetime interest in storytelling began when I was a little girl dreaming up tales and running hand in hand with my first best friend. I had no idea then that I would spend my professional life telling women's stories through films. While producing *Little Women* in 1993, I invited Nancy Lindemeyer, then editor of *Victoria* magazine, to visit the set in Vancouver, Canada. We shared mugs of tea in the hectic location office and laughed together about its refreshing quality despite the lack of ceremony. Over the course of these afternoons, we discovered that we were both passionately interested in the lives of women—and the things that matter most to them.

When Nancy asked me to write a foreword to this book, my thoughts reeled back to Kit Shannon, my first best friend. Her name always conjured up a heroine from an old folk song or fairy tale. Her large Irish family seemed just that magical and exotic in the surroundings of our San Fernando Valley elementary school. In fifth grade, when we were separated and placed in different classes, Kit and I decided to arrange a weekly play date. We were determined to keep our friendship going.

I remember that every Wednesday, I would forget to meet her at the school gate, walking home in a daze only to be reminded by my heartsick mother of my forgetfulness. My mother knew that Kit, who was as gentle and sensitive as herself, would be worried. I would then

Nancy Lindemeyer

run back the three blocks to find Kit waiting patiently. I would quickly grab her hand and run back home with her. She never complained; she never held it against me. I think she knew it was just the way I was, and it had nothing to do with my feelings for her.

Kit had to remind me many times to bring home a math book or turn in a paper, and always delighted in the crazy stories I would make up. (My daydreaming was often in overdrive, when I should have been paying attention in class.) I had the sense even then that she appreciated what was really important. Kit had wisdom beyond her years. It would take me much longer to reach her level of maturity.

I especially remember how her wonderful Irish immigrant father spent weeks refurbishing and painting an old bike as a present for her birthday. When we both saw it for the first time, there were tears of joy in her eyes. I knew it was because she understood how hard her father had worked to please her   not that the bicycle itself was anything particularly special. Kit rode it proudly beside my brand new Schwinn with the sparkle paint and longhorn handlebars. Somehow we both realized that she was very lucky.

When we went to different junior high schools, we drifted apart and lost touch. But more than forty years later, my memory of Kit is still as vivid and meaningful to me as ever. Her unconditional friendship, her kindness, and the warmth of her family were lessons that left an indelible imprint on me.

What is clear from the stories in this book is that nearly all women have planted deep in their hearts and minds such seemingly taken-for-granted little friends—mirror images in which their own self-image begins to take place. However far we travel in life, we remain close to the roots of our childhood. As you become acquainted with the women whose stories are told here, you will inevitably be carried back to your own youth and recall the freshness of that once-in-a-lifetime first friendship.

Denise Di Novi

Introduction

The first day of school, the year I was seven, I ran down the newly painted steps of our house, an old Connecticut Victorian on Stratford Avenue, anxious to start classes. That summer had gone quickly, and I had had little time to look for chums. The Babcock family lived next door, and one of their daughters and I spent some time together, but we were not to be in the same grade or even in the same school. My father had recently married for the second time, after my mother's death two years before. Bringing together a family was not easy, nor did it go smoothly.

My sister, ten years older, still grieved the life she had known. My father devoted himself to working as hard as he could to provide for us all and make new beginnings. My stepmother enlisted her mother in the process of raising us.

On that day, on the corner of Sixth Street, I met Janice Foster, and we walked to school—our first walk of many in the days, months, and years to come. Our destination was the brick building on the corner of Central Avenue where for years Sadie Caldwell had been principal. I already knew Miss Caldwell and her reputation because she was a member of our church, which stood just kitty-corner from the school. Janice had already spent three years in the drafty old schoolrooms. Their tall windows looked out on the friendly little library across the street. The dreaded cloakrooms were dark and

Nancy Lindemeyer

Nancy (right) and Janice on Easter wearing white gloves and new coats.

inhospitable to the "talkers," who had to spend time incarcerated with the coats and umbrellas.

Perhaps it was because Janice was a veteran of Lincoln School that I bonded with her on that September day. I don't remember what was so special about our original attachment. Our fathers, I was to discover, were boyhood acquaintances. Harry Foster, who was the manager of our local movie house, told me sometime later that he and my dad had been "doughnutnappers" in their boyhood days. On the way to school, they would whittle long sticks to arrowlike points, and then "bag" succulent doughnuts from Mrs. Vinka's Hungarian Bakery as they cooled by open windows in the early morning hours. When I first heard this story, as a well-brought-up child, I was horrified. Looking back, I suspect that Mrs. Vinka knew the capers of generations of lads and considered it the cost of doing business.

Janice and I spent countless hours together in and out of class. When we walked home together, I would often stop in at her apartment on the ground floor of a six-unit building. Her mother was often not feeling well, and we would spend time at her feet as she rested in a chair in the living room. The year we were ten, Mrs. Foster died, and Janice and I began to share not only the intimacies of Miss Baker's fourth grade but a grown-up loneliness as well.

As childhood days gathered around us with their share of backyard picnics, days at the beach, birthday parties, Easter mornings, and Christmas Eves, we outgrew Lincoln School and started the even longer walk along Central Avenue up the hill to Harding High School. The summer before we were to enroll in ninth grade, we took pictures of ourselves on the steps. The grins on our faces belied our excitement as we entered this momentous stage in our lives. We could hardly wait to begin. What we didn't realize was how much this new era would separate us. Going to college had become the singular preoccupation of my life; Janice was preparing for business courses. We would no longer be sharing classes and teachers, and new friends would begin to share our time and interests.

After graduation we lost touch. But at the beginning of every school year, as September light fell on my face for the first time, I would think back, seeing myself as the lonely, awkward child with too-long legs heading up the street to meet a darling girl with an adorable pug nose and hair brushed into ringlets of shining curls, both of us hustling off on the brink of a first best friendship.

Years and years later, I found Janice again. As a writer and magazine editor, I had told our tale several times in print, always hoping she might see it and contact me. Instead, a high school reunion and the Internet united us again. When the email came back from her, she simply said, "Oh, Nancy."

Our story is the inspiration for this book about first best friends. Janice was the guest at the first birthday party I remember. I can taste Harry Foster's famous egg salad sandwiches. And the day I collapsed a lawn chair is recorded in a photo that came out of Jan's archive, proving once again why I was not a star pupil, like Janice, at Miss Virginia's dancing school. We were in Girl Scouts together, and she reveres my stepmother's influence in her life as the scout leader who took us to Washington, D.C.—her first real trip—to say nothing of tasting Chinese food with my family in New York City. Janice went camping with us and ate the first fish she ever caught roasted on an open fire: "The best taste of my life," she says. Hearing these recollections was

Nancy Lindemeyer

especially poignant to me because my stepmother and I always had a clash of wills, and our relationship had its troubling aspects. How she would enjoy knowing that her energy and enthusiasm affected Janice's life, as well as those of the other girls she shepherded. It gives me a renewed pride in a woman whose gifts to me took years of maturity to appreciate. Janice's memory bank includes a conversation with my marvelous Italian grandfather, who always welcomed my school friends on Saturday with a freshly made pot of minestrone and invited them to sniff the basil from his garden. "My Nancy is thirteen going on thirty," he told Janice. Both of them doubtless agreed about my seriousness and my tendency to worry about everything.

What amazed me most was Janice's account of a surprise birthday party she gave me when I was probably about eight or nine. Janice and my family had kept the secret very well. On the day of the party, I was to go to her home after school, but as we walked home, that big old barn of Lincoln School just steps behind us, I announced that I had too much to do and could not stay and play that day. Janice held fast to the secret, and somehow my stepmother got me to reconsider my weighty duties, and the party and the surprise came off as planned. All who know me well, who have worked with me over the years, recognize that having too much to do to take time out for pleasure has been a lifetime curse.

Usually, my stepmother would not have countenanced parties for my birthday because it is the week before Christmas. I was often allowed to ask Janice and another friend or two for dinner to share my cake, but presents were discouraged because she felt that put an undue burden on parents at that time of year.

And what of the time that Janice paced nervously in our parlor while I went upstairs to change after a dusty playtime in the backyard? We were both eager to attend a school event. When I got to the bottom of the stairs (and this is Janice's memory, not mine), I looked down at my feet to discover that I had forgotten to change my socks. With an improvisational dispatch that later served me well in my magazine

Recent eighth-grade grads.

career, I sat on the bottom step, turned the offending socks inside out, and we hurried off to our fun. What a silly thing to remember all these years, and what a blessing to have someone in your life who does.

Our first best friendships are formed in innocence. There is the little girl next door with whom to walk to school, to giggle on the phone, and to exchange friendship bracelets and vows. Ask almost any woman about her first best friend, and you will most likely experience a moment of silence, then a burst of memories of what her childhood was like. For example, "the Barbie heist" is how one still slightly embarrassed woman describes the day she hauled off her friend's dolls because her own mom wouldn't let her have the more sophisticated Barbie. It's not only something to laugh about now but a tale that epitomizes a mother's unsuccessful attempt to impose her standards on a little girl with a mind of her own.

Many, many times these early couplings knit themselves into the fabric of lives lived in tandem. And sometimes there are unbridgeable separations and wounds that, for one reason or another, never heal. But first friendships will always be that time when birthday parties, bike rides, scout camps, playing after school, and sleepovers were the stuff of life.

Having asked dozens of women to share their first best friend experiences, I have found that all have many of the same ingredients, but each one has its defining moment. Two little girls live across the

Nancy Lindemeyer

hall from each other in a Washington suburb. They are natural playmates but become far more as, thirty years later, they plan a reunion halfway across the country, having never lost touch. "JoAnn remembers my father," says Bernadette. "No one else I know now does." Shared memories have made these two women more important to each other as the years go by. It is a strong reason for them to unite as their links to the past grow fewer and fewer and for JoAnn to travel from North Carolina to Minneapolis—"but not in the winter," Bernadette cautions her.

Many of us after high school and college lead hectic lives—and we take different paths from the people with whom we grew up. The obligatory Christmas and birthday cards may stop or come less frequently when careers, marriages, and children monopolize our lives. There comes a time when we again have the leisure and pleasure to know the one who meant so much to us on that Saturday afternoon trek to the movies. First best friends are falling into each other's arms again as high school and college reunions take place and the Internet brings us all closer together.

This book is a loving tribute to first best friends, because Janice has meant so much to me these past few years—as she did delicate decades ago. For those who have kept an unbroken thread over the years, this is a time to rejoice in good fortune. For those who seek to know again, there is the anticipation of wishes fulfilled. Whispers in the ear, hand in hand—as women we are girls again with those who chose us because they liked us first and who love all the things we have meant to each other.

Pillars

The first best friends who often met
at school over drawing paper and
crayons become bridesmaids, god-
mothers, and confidantes in lives that
stay forever entwined.

While they are certainly friends, they are more than that—they are longtime witnesses to each other's lives. They stand steadfast during the years since they skipped, jumped rope, and giggled at pizza parties and sleepovers. Without asking for notice, they are the pillars of our lives. "Sometimes they hold us up and sometimes they lean on you," as one wise woman so beautifully and simply stated.

It is a lovely gift to go through life with this special person of your choosing, as the stories in this section illustrate. Here, you'll learn about the day they first met, and you'll ofton laugh and be touched by the journey they have taken together. Perhaps you will recognize in their friendships moments from your own. You may want to celebrate the privilege of having such pillars for what it is—an eloquent bond that brings with it comfort, joy, and grace.

The Gold Standard
Par and Betsy

Betsy lived a long, rich, and rewarding life. She raised three accomplished sons, was a loving and adored wife, and had eleven grandchildren. As a devoted animal-rights activist, she was an outstanding head of the Animal Rescue Group in Washington, D.C., following in the footsteps of her mother. During her twenty-year tenure, she presided over building a new home for the facility and making it a model for other communities. Her own home might have as many as five dogs in residence at any one time, and often there were visiting animals awaiting adoption. But during the last three decades of Betsy's life, she missed her soul mate and childhood friend, Parthenia, who died too early.

"Mother never replaced her," said her son Peter. "We were taught to be very respectful of our parents' friends, and we never called them by first names, except for Par—she was special."

On the first day of kindergarten at Washington's Holton-Arms School, a girl whom Par was to describe in one of her delightful occasional poems as having straight dark hair, big brown eyes, and "the deepest dimples in the whole of town," was a shy but reassuring presence for her. Par's daughter Virginia said, "My mother arrived at her first day of school a bit late, and the teacher decided that Elizabeth Simpson was to be Parthenia's designated friend—and in no uncertain terms, it seems." Par, an only child, had this unusual

Par (left) and Betsy—a loving friendship began in kindergarten.

first name, as well as a string of second and third names and a many-lettered last name. While others in the class might have found it amusing and off-putting, it mattered not at all to Betsy, not then nor ever.

After graduation from Holton-Arms, Par went off to Sarah Lawrence College, and Betsy worked in her father's medical office. These were the years when the women were not in close daily contact, but that was to change when both of their marriages brought them near each other in the Spring Valley neighborhood of northwest Washington. That is when "the ritual" began.

Every weekday, the two women went out to lunch at friendly nearby restaurants. "Before the lunch date," says Par's younger daughter, Cynthia, "there was a rather lengthy phone conversation." Par had a literary bent and wrote refreshing poems about many aspects of her life. In one, she referred to Betsy as a twin—"as close as a fish is to a fin." At the time the poem was written, the friendship had endured for twenty-seven years, "with never a cross or angry day." The poem does make a fleeting reference to a contested croquet game, and Virginia remembers that there was a dispute when the women were about twelve. "At that point," Virginia affirms, "they decided to never argue or disagree again. And they never did."

Par and Betsy (who became Buffy after one of Par's daughters

Par in a beautiful formal portrait taken for her debut.

so called her) were so close that they actually invented a language of their own. They named it "Pansy talk," after a dog Buffy had at the time. "It was an odd-accented purring affair that they continued to use into adulthood and was accompanied with lots of laughter," remembers Virginia. To Cynthia, "it was just their way, not designed to keep things from any of the rest of us. I never saw doors closed or heard whispers when my mother and Betsy were together. They simply delighted in each other, and I think the relationship worked so well because they both respected each other's life." Cynthia also remembers that her mother, in particular, had nicknames for almost everyone, especially Betsy, who was sometimes referred to as Madame Binks.

Betsy's son Peter says his mother never complained about presiding over an all-male bastion as her three boys, who played football, went through childhood and adolescence in stair-step fashion. Friends and neighbors recall Betsy's household, in contrast to Par's more organized and formal home (which reflected her passion for Victoriana), as a beehive abuzz with boys and dogs, as well as a minefield of ever-present sports gear and dog bowls. "She was a very feminine woman yet accepted all the football cleats and

Nancy Lindemeyer

sports talk around the dinner table as a matter of course," says Peter. "I think having Par to relate to, go shopping for hats with, to lunch with, was a wonderful respite for her." Both sets of children found the relationship of "the twins" enriching and, over the years, the source of family lore. Betsy's ungainly dog Jumbo, named for Barnum's famous elephant, did not take well to strangers, or even to family members at times, sending the boys scurrying behind their bedroom doors occasionally. But he was a docile, lovable puppy as far as Par was concerned. Even a temperamental dog, if he was Betsy's, could do no wrong in Par's eyes.

"Mother was a marvelous cook," says Peter, "but not Par. We don't know how she did it, but her husband never realized that she imported her Thanksgiving dinner every year from a nearby restaurant."

Cynthia confirms the secret: "Mummy would be out in the kitchen making all kinds of appropriate motions, so Dad never caught on." Looking at the matter from outside the family, one has to wonder if a kind husband chose to look the other way and enjoy his pumpkin pie from Hot Shoppes.

> *Constant use had not worn ragged the fabric of their friendship.*
>
> Dorothy Parker, "The Standard of Living"

These years were "delicious and heartwarming" times for both families, according to Cynthia. "Mummy and Buffy are my role models for friendships. I don't know anything different than the genuine respect these two women had for each other. They taught me about giving and receiving and how to have marvelous relationships with women in your life. I believe they finessed the art of active lives, rich marriages (both adored their husbands), family, friendship, and loyalty. The two of them were part of the fabric of our lives in the best possible ways."

When Betsy and her husband traveled in the late 1960s, Par wrote a poem that told of her loneliness "without the comfort of talk, talk, talk." She was one "who finds no joy wherever she seeks / For her twin has departed for 7 weeks."

Betsy was to return, of course. A decade later, after a long illness, it was Par who left her friend. For the last three months of Par's life, Betsy sat at her bedside every day, sometimes having to walk through snowdrifts to get there. Virginia has lovely memories of their final days together. "They never talked about Mummy's dying. I would often try to leave them alone, but if I came back early, I would find them gossiping, laughing, and cheering each other. Sometimes, they were just quiet and holding hands. I think when my mother died, it was the greatest loss to Buffy because they were part of each other's every day with such deep affection."

Betsy remained in the lives of Par's girls—Cynthia was in her twenties and Virginia just thirty when their mother died—and Par's grandchildren to follow, until her death at age ninety. "Buffy was my godmother, and she tended to us just as my mother would have wanted her to," says Virginia, who also noted that while one might be tempted to pry a secret from the past, the women's loyalty oath to each other held fast. It was Virginia who discovered her mother's poems discreetly placed in a dresser drawer. They are a memoir of a unique friendship and are truly a family treasure. It is said that new friends are silver but old friends are gold. If that is so, Par and Madame Binks lived as friends of the finest gold standard.

Nancy Lindemeyer

Betsy, as lovely as described in one of Par's poems, about eighteen years old.

"A BON VOYAGE FOR 7 WEEKS"

written by Par to Betsy, June 15, 1967

Who is that wraith with step so slow

Whose back is bent, whose head is low,

Whose toothy smile and carefree air

Have changed into a mournful stare,

Who wanders, sadly, store to store,

Exuding grief from every pore,

Who chews a solitary stalk

Without the comfort of talk, talk, talk,

Whose zest for sales and the perfect buy

Has been replaced by a wrenching sigh,

Who finds no joy wherever she seeks—

For her twin has departed for 7 weeks!

"You'll Be Fine"
Katie and Shannon

In early June the farms in Central Iowa are a study in green—the corn plants are splashed with a sunny yellow, and the soybeans take on a deep, rich velvet green. Peonies bloom around porches, and kitchen gardens are just coming into their own, friendly little patches dwarfed by the huge expanses of crops. Days are pleasant without being sultry, and nights are still cool and sweet. It's before the heat that makes the crops grow profusely and pesters the folks at picnics, and before summer band concerts take hold. (Iowans, by the way, don't like to be asked about the weather in July—an old saw from *The Music Man*.) It's a perfect time for a wedding and a lovely time for two young women to celebrate another milestone in their lives.

On the steps of the Catholic church in Colfax, Shannon, her eight attendants clad in the softest blue, and her mom and dad waited patiently for the ceremony to begin. "It was a perfect day," says Shannon, "and one of the most precious moments that will always stand out in my mind is thinking then how lucky I was to have such a great family and friends around me. And of course, there was Katie. I knew I could count on her, as I always have, to keep me calm. She's great at that, to tell me, 'You'll be fine.'"

Both Katie and Shannon were reared on Iowa farms smack in the middle of the state. Being friends as farm girls is different from having a playmate on your block in the suburbs or in a town or city,

Nancy Lindemeyer

not to mention on the same floor in your apartment building. Not only does getting together mean more coordination for parents, but the kinds of activities that challenge children are considerably different. City kids dream and read about having horses to ride and tend; farm kids can actually have them, along with 4-H projects that involve sheep and pigs!

It was in the second grade, at the Colfax-Mingo Consolidated School, that Katie and Shannon became soul mates. "Our wise teacher assigned us to share a reading barrel: little carrels, with space for two children to be quiet and read together," Shannon remembers. "In that cozy setting, we both discovered that not only did we love to read, but we were crazy about horses." Each begged for a horse of her own, and in fifth grade, Shannon was to have hers, a quarter horse named Cisco. "The name came from Lt. John Dunbar's horse in the film *Dances with Wolves*. My parents took me to see the movie, and when the horse dies in the middle, I screamed bloody murder. I guess I wanted to bring that horse back to life again."

"I was really quite jealous at the time," admits Katie, "but in a couple more years, I had my Appaloosa. These horses are so beautiful, having leopard-spotted coats, and they were developed by the Nez Perce Indians in the Pacific Northwest. But when you have an animal of your own on a farm, it's up to you to take care of it. And Shannon and I both discovered in time that it was more fun to think and read about horses and admire them in films like *The Man from Snowy River* than actually ride and be responsible for them." When Shannon was thrown from her horse, she was only slightly hurt but she was so shaken that she decided never to ride again.

But the girls were not entirely through with tending animals. Like many rural kids, they were active members of a 4-H club. While these clubs are designed to teach the rudiments of farm life to youngsters, as well as to keep them interested in farming as a way of life, they also aim to develop the youngsters' heads, hearts, hands, and health. "Katie raised sheep, and I raised pigs," Shannon relates matter-of-factly, as if she were talking about working on a scout badge about identifying birdcalls. "For several years we took our animals to the Jasper County Fair in nearby Newton, but we didn't make it to the state fair in Des Moines. No ribbons for us."

Because the girls lived on opposite sides of town, they did not spend that much time at each other's homes. There were sleepovers, but most of their togetherness happened in and around school. In middle school, they were heavily involved in the Spanish Club and a host of community and service projects. "We both played trumpet in the school band, taking the positions of first and second chair. At one concert we cooked up the idea of trading measures. I took the first bar, and when I lowered my horn, Shannon played the second, and so forth." When a new band instructor came to school and a new trumpet player took the first chair, the magic of being in the band wore off for Katie and Shannon, and they put down their trumpets for good.

The girls never doubted, nor did their parents, that they would go to Iowa State University in Ames. It was less than an hour from home, so in addition to getting to sleep in their own beds often and eat their moms' Sunday dinners, they were joined by their families at Cyclone football games and other campus activities. "Of course we were roommates," the women chime in together. "We are typical Iowans, we don't hold grudges or wear our feelings on our sleeves. So we never had even a tiny misunderstanding, including after college when we continued to live together. Shannon is more affectionate than I am, but we are on the same laugh meter," says Katie, who now works for her school's alumni association.

While Shannon is not truly "in" farming, she is still of it. The former zoology major works as a laboratory technician in the seed development area of a large agricultural company. Wade, the groom who was waiting at the front of the church that June day, is the director of the student farm at a local community college. The couple met the summer after they both graduated from college. "We bonded over our love of bologna-and-potato-chip sandwiches," Shannon

Nancy Lindemeyer

jokes, "and were engaged eleven months after we started dating. The first person we shared our joy with was Katie. She hugged me tight and told me how happy she was for me."

"Wade is a great husband for Shannon, and I'm happy that they are still close by. Even so, we email or talk on the phone every day. We are ready to continue our friendship wherever it takes us," Katie adds.

The pale blue bridesmaid dresses hang in closets now, and the roses and hydrangeas and blue delphiniums of the bouquets will fade from memory as the years go by. The tears shed when Shannon danced with her dad will always be especially poignant for Katie, because she knows how close the two are. One of the H's in the 4-H clover leaf symbol stands for *heart*, and the refrain of the club's song refers to pledging "my heart to greater loyalty." Shannon and Katie have done that, with pigs and sheep and horses in attendance.

If you're ever in a jam, here I am.
If you ever need a pal, I'm your gal. . . .
It's friendship, friendship,
Just a perfect blendship.
When other friendships have been forgot,
Ours will still be hot.

Cole Porter, "Friendship"

Family Ties

Nancy and Betty

M aking one's way through the generational connections between
Nancy's family and Betty's is like trying to untangle the begats
in the book of Genesis. The most recent event: Betty's granddaughter
is getting married in the Basketball Hall of Fame, in Springfield,
Massachusetts, and all of Nancy's family are headed there from
Connecticut. "My granddaughters have been in the weddings of all
Betty's grandchildren," says Nancy, remembering the little girl she
encountered on the corner of her street when they were both seven.

Bridgeport, Connecticut, is Nancy's hometown. When she was
growing up on Long Island Sound, most of the homes in her neighborhood were inhabited by folks in better economic circumstances
than hers. In fact, there were a few millionaires' mansions, and
Nancy loved being invited to some of them for lawn parties à la *The
Great Gatsby*. "I used to go to the corner of my street every day to
meet my dad as he came home from work," reports Nancy. One day
there was a surprising sight. "I remember it like it was yesterday,"
says the lively, cheerful woman, who delights in every minute with
her family and friends—including old ones from both grammar and
high school. Case in point: a monthly luncheon with "the girls from
Harding High."

There was Betty, an apparition in clothes that attracted Nancy's
attention immediately: "Really nice things, nothing like what the kids

I palled around with wore." What was this astonishing outfit? "Black Watch–tartan wool skirt, a dark green cardigan over a very white blouse, and knee socks." While Nancy was caught in her astonishment, Betty spoke first. "She had come to live with the four spinster sisters and their mother, who resided on the very next corner. Of course, we became friends right away. She played at my house, and I at hers, which was much fancier. I shared a bedroom with my sister, but Betsy had her own in a home with elegant furnishings, such as Tiffany lamps. I was fascinated by the mysterious back staircase designed for a maid to scurry about behind the scenes."

Eyebrows were raised about four unmarried women, all in their thirties, and their mother adopting a seven-year-old girl. "The explanation we were given was that Betty had been brought up in an orphanage in Upstate New York," says Nancy. "Her new sisters and my dad and his three sisters had grown up together and were good friends. Even so, my family was baffled by Betty's sudden arrival. Soon, however, she was just another child in the neighborhood, and how she got there was not top of mind."

When second grade began, both the girls were in Mrs. Hay's class at Newfield School. Since they went home for lunch, there were four chatty walks together every day. Even when they later went to different schools, they still stayed close but, naturally, spent less and less time together. Then Nancy went off to college; Betty did not. But the friends who began with a mysterious chance meeting were destined to live near each other again as young married women.

"We saw each other every day, and Betty would call me so often I had to tell her I couldn't spend so much time on the phone—I wasn't getting anything else done! We both still laugh about it. We didn't have very much money to spare in the beginning of our marriages, so we invented ways to make things seem better than they actually were. For one, we traded curtains at the beginning of each season so it would look like we had new ones. And we borrowed all sorts of household things to stretch our inventories. We were pretty ingenious, I think," says Nancy these many years later. Now she lives in a venerable Connecticut town that spells New England, from the manicured green to the spired churches. "My dad used to drive us to the country every Sunday, and I dreamed of living in one of the cozy houses we passed slowly by. The floors can be a little askew, but you lose your heart to the utter charm of the place."

The mystery of Betty's adoption was solved when it was revealed later in her life that one of her adopted sisters was, in truth, her mother. In time, all of the women married and had children. "We babysat and took care of them all. When our own kids were old enough, they babysat for the children of the children of Betty's mother and aunts. Now Betty has been taking care of two of my granddaughters since they were three months old. My first best friend and her husband are just like another set of grandparents, and we are all thrilled at how this somewhat complicated tangle has evolved. We often tell the girls some of the zany things we did when we were their ages—and bring them into our ever-widening circle."

"Betty and I live totally different lifestyles, but we still talk every day—at least once! We are delighted with how closely related our families are, especially on occasions like weddings. We let each other be who we are but are always there for support when needed, which has been quite often—mostly Betty taking care of me. There is nothing we don't know about each other's life. It's so good to talk to her about when we were kids—about my mother, who died when I was thirteen, my father, and her real mother. I don't know what I would do without Betty."

The girl in the Black Watch–tartan skirt found more than a chum on that street corner in Bridgeport. She and Nancy have raised their tribes to love one another for their shared history and to be present in the years to come. Family ties, to be sure.

Nancy Lindemeyer

No Friend Like a Sister
Kathleen and Sheila

"I never wanted to leave her side," says Kathleen, as she remembers the time when her little sister, younger by fifteen months, was recovering from having her tonsils out. She was a "brave little soul," and Kathleen sat by her parents' bed, where the patient was allowed to spend days having ice cream lovingly fed to her by her big sis.

The girls were middle children in a family of five girls and one boy. "I never needed to look for a friend outside the family, and I don't have a memory that does not include Sheila," Kathleen relates. There was never any jealousy or other not-so-sisterly behavior between the two of them. Sisters can have their sibling rivalries, and sometimes it takes growing up to truly enjoy the closeness of being from the same family. Kathleen and Sheila needed no such period of adjustment.

"We were naughty together, and we thought we faced a spanking from our dad. We decided to pad the anticipated blows by putting on all the panties we owned. He did make us return to the scene of the crime and apologize, but the panty caper was in vain. He didn't spank us. I think from that time on, we made an unspoken compact to protect each other. We'd be partners, whatever that meant."

This did not mean that Kathleen relinquished her older-sister role. On Sheila's first day of kindergarten, she had a quite serious fall on her walk home from school. "I was waiting for her at the corner of our city block in Chicago when the little girl who was with her came rushing up to tell me that Sheila was hurt. Bleeding profusely from a head injury, she was rushed to the hospital. Dad had to come home from work, it was so serious, and it was the first time in my life that anyone in my family had a brush with harm. Sheila was again so brave, and I came to realize what an incredible little person had been born into my life."

Each friend represents a world in us,
a world possibly not born until they arrive,
and it is only by this meeting
that a new world is born.

Anais Nin

When the family moved from Chicago to a nearby suburb, Kathleen ran into school problems, and it was Sheila who "showed her true stripes as a friend." It was the beginning of sixth grade, and Kathleen realized that her new schoolmates found her different, being from the bigger city. "I was teased and bullied, not invited to parties, and even received crank calls. It was devastating to me and my family. Sheila understood the devastating damage to my young heart and pride. I will always love her for what her loyalty meant to me during what were several terribly hurtful years. Fortunately, grammar school ended, and so did all this childish nonsense. I survived with Sheila's hand in mine."

Both sisters went off to the same college in Mobile, Alabama. In Sheila's freshman year, there was a fierce hurricane, and all students were told to remain in their own dorms. "But we both knew we

Nancy Lindemeyer

needed to be together, so Sheila climbed out one of her windows, braved the wind and rain, and found her way to my room. Even Mother Nature couldn't keep us apart."

After college, Kathleen and Sheila were again under the same roof, as roommates. "My judgment in boyfriends was sometimes challenged," confesses Kathleen, "and Sheila gave me some pretty good advice that, luckily, I followed, if reluctantly at times. But she always had my best interests at heart and wasn't afraid to risk our relationship to tell me what she thought."

Kathleen did have a failed first marriage, the first in her devout Irish Catholic family. "Sheila listened when it was clear that I had a tough decision to make and never placed any blame, either on me or my husband. She was the beacon in the family, and while it was difficult for them, they followed her lead in understanding and support." Now both sisters have strong marriages and kids off at college.

"When Sheila's Ryan left for college, I saw how that separation affected her, and I started to prepare myself for when our only son, Will, would leave home, too. It did help to understand that, while there is no real guide to how to control one's emotions when the inevitable happens, you do get through it, just like Sheila did."

When Kathleen's cell phone rings, as it so often does—she's in magazine advertising—and she sees that it's Sheila, she takes a deep breath and immediately smiles. Her naughty partner in crime, her stalwart defender in grammar school, her wise and kind adviser in affairs of the heart, her first best friend, her little sister is on the line, and it feels so good. Kathleen is proud and happy that she chose someone in her own backyard.

Finders Keepers

Finding a worthy opponent.

As meaningful

(sometimes the same)

as finding a friend.

A soul mate,

opposite you,

playing Scrabble, jacks, boxball.

A meeting of minds.

A battle over ability.

The weapon?

The letter z.

Or a little rubber ball.

Friendship here

took on dimension.

Evenly matched.

Beautifully the same and opposite.

Borg & McEnroe.

Ali & Frazier.

The Red Sox & Yankees.

You and your friend,

chewing on a ponytail,

plotting a steely superiority.

You needed her,

loved her,

were bound to her

for eternity.

You had told her

your secrets.

Her tears had fallen on your argyle sweater.

But now you wanted to annihilate her,

your almost-sister,

with a little help from Parker Brothers.

—Robin Reiser

Building Bridges
Sue and Kath

The Golden Gate Bridge spans a mile-wide strait between San Francisco and Marin County. By any standard of architecture and engineering, it's a wonder of the world, placed in a majestic natural setting. Enthusiasts sing its praises for its strength, purpose, and Art Deco design. For those who cross it, it's either an inspiration or a maddening rush-hour bottleneck. Sue lives on the San Francisco end, Kath at the other, and they think of it not so much as separating them but as being another bridge to each other. They have kept a promise they made as youngsters growing up in Des Moines, Iowa, shortly after Kath met Sue for the first time when she noticed her picking flowers.

Sue and Kath lived in an area of substantial homes, some from the late nineteenth century, including Terrace Hill, now the home of the governor of Iowa. Trees tower over houses with pillared porches, parlors, and well-mannered gardens. Sue was the youngest in her family of four kids—two sisters and a brother—Kath was the oldest in hers. The girls, who started out together in the same kindergarten class, were intentionally and wisely separated in first grade by the sisters at St. Augustine, but that didn't stop them from being close pals—almost as if they were siblings. "We made a pact," says Sue, "vowing when we grew up we would always live next door to each other and our houses would be

Nancy Lindemeyer

Sue (right) and Kath—vacationing at a favorite lake.

connected by a bridge. I guess we made that sort of happen, by living on either end of the Golden Gate!"

"We did look alike. In fact, my own sister is petite and dark, while Sue and I are taller and blond," says Kath. "But that was deceptive, as we are very different in many, many ways. I have always been like a second-hand Rose when it comes to dressing, but Sue, even as a kid, had a perfect classic style. We've just had a friends gathering back in Des Moines, and I marveled how chic Sue looked in her white stylish sundress as I tramped around in well-worn sandals. When we were kids, I desperately wanted us to wear the same things, and Sue always resisted, maintaining what has always been her independent streak. Once, somehow, I was able to replicate an outfit Sue wore, which included not only a brown suede coat but matching helmet-style hat and mittens. When Sue saw me, she flatly said she hated this outfit—a hand-me-down, as it turned out—and would have gladly given it to me if I had told her I wanted it."

Kath became a nurse, married young, and has four children. Sue went on to study design, worked successfully in New York for Clinique cosmetics and as the art and creative director of *Victoria* magazine. To the latter she brought a sensibility honed by a lifetime of making aesthetic choices, reining in excesses when the magazine tended in that direction. Expression with simplicity is her stock in

Sue (right) and Kath on the day of their first communion.

trade, not only in her dress but in her home as well. In Sue's kitchen, one is likely to find a beautiful hand-blown white-wine glass and a small bunch of white grapes on a counter. "But Sue sure is a good eater," Kath says. "I still envy her ability to pound down chili dogs without gaining weight."

On the other hand, Kath gets points for being an incredible cook. "I've admired what a great baker she is," says Sue. "Those giant cookies of hers have been sent to college campuses all over the country where her own children and nieces and nephews have resided."

"Unlike me, Sue has never been one to let you know how she is feeling. Her words have been as spare as her sense of style. But in the last few years, I've seen Sue opening up more, making what has always been a common place we shared even more meaningful for me," relates Kath. As good friends do, they have stood by each other in good times and bad, but it has sometimes pained Kath to see Sue struggle by herself. "It was her way, though, and I have always understood that."

Nancy Lindemeyer

Their friends always say that to know Sue is to know Kath. It won't be long in a conversation before one or the other is mentioning the longtime friend from childhood days in Des Moines. But it wasn't by design, they both insist, that they have lived near each other on both coasts over the years. Not long ago, Sue was sitting in a San Francisco restaurant with Kath's mom, who asked, "Could you ever have imagined we would be here tonight when we were all back in Des Moines and you and Kath were in and out of each house all the time?" Certainly, Sue says, she finds it incredible that for over forty years the girls who held hands on the day they took Holy Communion have had lifelong ties in seen and unseen ways. (Kath recalls that, on the day they were confirmed, Sue, in a style-conscious gesture, insisted on *not* turning down her lace-trimmed anklets.)

Sue now works in an architecture and design firm in which Kath's brother John is a partner. "I was at Kath's the day he was born," Sue muses, almost in amazement. "She's my oldest son's godmother," says Kath, "and Sue's always welcomed him into her life and home as she did recently when her perfect abode was inhabited by about five of us spread all over the place. It didn't seem to bother her a bit. And of course she never forgets his birthday. They have a special communication."

This year, when Sue's January birthday rolled around, Kath was traveling, intending to get back to San Francisco for a brunch at Sue's. As a little girl, Sue always asked that her birthday cake be prepared from a mix—a white box cake with canned chocolate frosting. And so she has always been indulged in what seemed a modest request that was easy for Kath to honor. Once, when Kath hosted a party in a chic restaurant, she had to pay a cutting fee for the humble cake she had baked and brought with her. It was something of a travesty for this renowned baker, but she did it happily for her first best friend. Kath feared that, for this birthday, she wouldn't be back in time to make the cake, so she enlisted a friend to bake and deliver it. "You can't know how much this goes against my grain," said the stand-in baker friend. "I'd loved to have made a marvelous one for the occasion."

No matter, this longtime ritual, as simple as it seems, is a light-hearted and loving way to express a deep-seated and caring connection. In many ways, Sue and Kath do live next door to each other—and the bridge between their houses is strong, well trodden, and always open to new life experiences. They both claim the Golden Gate as the symbol of that promise they made as little girls in Des Moines. They travel it frequently, always looking forward to seeing each other—and never surprised at what the other will be wearing.

Star Bright

Vera and Teuta

Robi started college this year. He's a good student who wants to be an architect or engineer. With several scholarships on the horizon, he chose Clarkson University, in Potsdam, New York. His mother sent him off with a good down parka for the harsh upstate winters and the bittersweet tears all moms shed when the firstborn takes wing. There is pride in accomplishments and a touch of sadness that things will never be exactly the same again. "I am so happy to see him following his dreams," says the stately woman who came with Robi to America when he was ten months old, seeking asylum from war-torn Montenegro. Among the things that Robi has taken with him is a memorial card he is never without.

"Just think," Vera told her son as she said good-bye to him, "how proud Teuta would be of you now." This is a time when neither they nor Robi's sister, Christina, can leave out of their thoughts their mother's friend who helped raise them. Five years ago, at age thirty, Teuta suffered a heart attack and died as Robi and Christina, merely children, desperately tried to save her. It was an experience that the family still deals with—a tragedy of the loss of a loving, vibrant woman who lived every day to its fullest. "It was how she thought of things," says Vera. "She loved my kids as if they were her own. Oh, how I miss our cup of coffee together every day when I came home from work."

Vera and Teuta became friends as girls, when they met at a family wedding, but it was in their first year of high school that their closeness really began. Both were excellent students, and they walked to school along rugged roads in their native Tuzi, often dodging snakes. "It is a small place," Vera says. "Our parents were farmers, and it was a very difficult life, especially with the political conditions in the country. We were ethnic Albanians in a place that was not the country of our ancestors. We were poor, but we managed to have fun together—often sleeping at each other's home. Because of us, our families became very close. I remember the Christmases we celebrated together as being especially happy times. What I always admired about Teuta was that she never dwelt on the negatives of life."

Coming to America to escape the wars in her country was a wonderful thing for Vera and her children. However, life in a new country did not heal the wounds in her marriage, which ended several years later. Teuta came to the United States a few years after Vera as an employee of the United Nations, assigned to Michigan. When she came to New York to visit Vera, she decided to stay in a place she loved almost at first sight. From that point on, Teuta lived with Vera, helping the single mother care for her children. "She was like a second mother to Robi and Christina, and they loved her with all their hearts. She spoiled them, too. But I didn't mind. She was their fairy godmother."

All of Vera's immediate family eventually came to America, and now her mother and several other relatives live across the street from her. Teuta was always embraced as another daughter. "When my mother cooked something special for dinner, she would save a healthy portion for Teuta. I can see her putting foil over the plate, putting it in the fridge, and warning everyone not to touch it." It was Teuta's father who said it beautifully when Vera visited him a few years ago in Tuzi: "Vera, when I see you, I see that you are half Teuta. She lives in you now."

Nancy Lindemeyer

"We saw each other as a star," Vera says. "We each shined for the other, but she always put me highest in the sky." While the loss of Teuta will always be deep in the hearts of Vera, Robi, and Christina, they have worked very hard to remember that she would have wanted them to enjoy life, the way she did. She would want Robi to succeed in college and would be his cheerleader, according to Vera.

"I have a happy life in so many ways," Vera affirms. "Teuta never met my new husband, but I know she would approve. I have just bought the business where I worked for eight years—an accomplishment both of us dreamed about when we came to a country that opened up such opportunities for us. We believed in working hard; but we never wanted to sacrifice the enjoyment of life along the way. I am so happy that we lived with this philosophy. And my kids have grown up surrounded by love and encouragement. But I will never forget Teuta."

Teuta left this family an incomparable legacy. Robi will keep her memorial card close to him, but it is in the depth of his heart that his mother's faithful friend will stay forever. When he shares good times with his family, she will be included. And if there are trials to come, there is a wisdom and philosophy of life to guide him. For Vera, Teuta, her friend from across the seas, remains her brightest star held highest.

Complementary

The bonds begun in childhood do not fray
for these first best friends, even when life
ushers them from the sandbox to larger
and more crowded stages. They mark the
milestones in each other's lives—and
find time to be together, often planning
meetings long in advance for holidays
or special birthdays.

Lives

These are the friends we will never do without, even if daily life keeps us apart and sometimes years go by without our seeing each other. The love and devotion we once shared continues to thrive in mind and spirit, and there are times when missing this first best friend proves so compelling that phone calls, emails, and visits follow.

In this section are tales of complementary lives that show how, through empathy, first best friendships survive and thrive in a busy world. These are the women whose lives have gone in different directions, yet they still relish visits to each other's homes and enjoy reading "the novel" in which their friend is the heroine. While they like to reminisce, they are also part of rich contemporary lives and take pride in each other's accomplishments. These are stories of women who have never forgotten what they shared when they were first best friends, doing everything side by side.

Born into Friendship
Ann and Phoebe

If the people of a community are lucky, they have a Bill Riley. In Des Moines, Iowa, for years this energetic radio and television personality threw his whole being into projects to make his town a more pleasant and exciting place to live. Bill was a diminutive guy, but he played as if he were indeed "as tall as an elephant's eye"—the measure of Iowa corn in good years. He became well known for the talent show he produced at the storied state fair—the one celebrated by Phil Stong's novel and the 1945 Rodgers and Hammerstein musical film that was based on it. Bill had such a following that he inspired two eight-year-old girls to put their wits together to raise funds for a zoo—a cause Bill was championing.

Ann and Phoebe were born a month apart—and into families who enjoyed a long and thriving friendship. "We have just been together all our lives," says Ann. It was no surprise for neighbors to see "the Ann and Phoebe team" going door-to-door borrowing every kid's beloved stuffed animals, taking them off pillows and out of playrooms. "We came up with the idea that we could create a zoo of our own, charge admission, and give Bill the money to get a real zoo," Ann remembers, still amazed that they pulled this off. "We staged the extravaganza in my parents' basement after we pushed aside the Ping-Pong table. Kids lined up with quarters, the price of admission. Bill got wind of what was going on, and we found our-

Nancy Lindemeyer

Ann (row 2, far left) and Phoebe (row 2, far right), the youngest girls in the dance recital.

selves on radio and TV. That was one of the great and good times."

"We were wonderfully creative together, with the zoo being one of the adventures I remember most from our collaborations. I always thought of us as Judy Garland and Mickey Rooney getting everybody together to put on a show," Phoebe recalls. Phoebe also treasures Ann's solo creativity. In high school, as a special tribute, Ann made a collage to celebrate all the attributes of her friend as well as many of the good times they had shared. Recently, Phoebe's mom found it in the family archive of her daughter's youth and sent it to her. "All over again, I wrote to thank Ann for her extreme thoughtfulness. It brought back so many good memories, it made me weepy."

Ballet classes were a rite of passage. "In the recital pictures, you always see Phoebe on one end of the cast and me on the other—for a time we were the youngest dancers, hanging in there." Ann and Phoebe also went off to sleepaway camp, where the girls were to learn to ride horses. "I didn't stick it out—I was horribly homesick," Ann says. "I did ride, but I think those horses went through their paces if kids were in the saddles or not." Later, she mustered up the courage to accompany Phoebe to camp in northern Minnesota. "I stood back and watched Phoebe become the star camper. Everyone liked her because she was so easy, a free spirit, playing guitar around the evening campfires." It was the beginning of Ann's appreciation of her

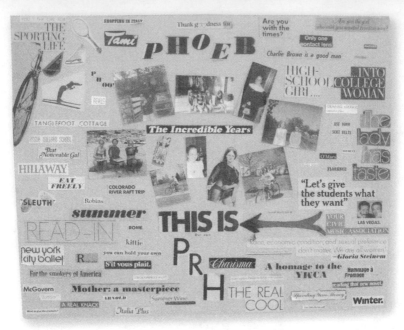

Ann's birthday tribute to her friend Phoebe, a collage made
in high school recalling so many good times together.

"wonderfully unusual" friend—with whom she had cast her lot from
the time both girls put their fingerprints in the fresh mortar when
Phoebe's parents were remodeling their home. "Phoebe's parents
have moved, but our prints are still there together for posterity!"

The two friends were not always perfect, admits Ann, who is now
a kindergarten teacher in Manhattan and understands mischief well.
"In one caper, we made a contraption out of spools of thread that we
used to rattle people's windows. Our parents insisted that we apologize to the folks we annoyed. We got a little of our own medicine one
day playing Ouija. We were at Phoebe's, one of the oldest houses in
the area, and the thought that it might be haunted was not hard for our
young imaginations to conjure up. While we were intent on the board,
a knock came at the door. When we went to answer, there was no one
there, and both of us ran for our lives, screaming at the top of our
lungs. We never found out who did it, but I suspect it was one of our
brothers, who knew how freaked we would be."

Nancy Lindemeyer

When Phoebe went to boarding school back East, for the first time Ann did not tag along. But joint family vacations continued, including one to the Grand Canyon when the girls were teenagers. "I began to see on that adventure on the Colorado River that my friend was such a caring person," says Ann, who recalls that Phoebe was especially kind to an older gentleman named Saul, who was probably not up to the rigors of the trip. "He was from Brooklyn, and I think he was wearing the first pair of blue jeans he ever owned. Phoebe was to keep in touch with him and Sam, the guide on the trip, for many years after." Ann has always been in awe of Phoebe's talent for friendship, a way of life that stems from a true and abiding interest in people. One of their rituals was the Christmas gathering when the girls and their families celebrated together. "We always called our favorite teacher from junior high. Ann Schluter was also our drama coach and seemed to take in stride some of our antics—like the time we all hid in the closet, bursting out to frighten her."

"I guess I was born into friendship," Ann muses. "I was so fortunate to have parents who practiced loving acts for others, and who welcomed the give and take that having important people in your life often requires. Phoebe was one of the people who watched me walk down the staircase in my parents' home on my wedding day, full-blown roses in my arms and such love in my heart. I wanted a home ceremony, and it had to be smaller than most, so everyone there was near and dear to me. The roaring fire was not the only warmth we all felt in that room, a frigid Valentine's Day. The fire was so robust that it cracked my mother's antique glass screen. She says she didn't mind because she always sees it as a reminder of my wedding day—the imperfection of a perfect memory. And recently, on our fiftieth birthdays, Phoebe and I and our moms celebrated together in New York, where I now live and work. Our moms traveled from Des Moines, and Phoebe came from Missoula, Montana, where she manages a photography studio. We went to the theater, had lovely dinners, shopped, and remembered all the birthdays we have had together. It happened to be the weekend of the Kentucky Derby, so we watched the race, sipped mint juleps, and joined in a rousing rendition of 'My Old Kentucky Home.' Phoebe, of course, who knew it by heart, led the chorus. Our lives have taken different paths, but who has had a life-long friend from babyhood? Not many, I suspect."

The Blank Zoo Park is now a Des Moines institution. Kids don't have to travel to Kansas City to see such attractions as a hissing cockroach, the mountain bongo, or a boa constrictor. Ann found herself working for the zoo again one summer—"watching the snake house for what seemed like endless hours."

She adds, "My dad took my son there for summer camp and for the Halloween tradition of 'Night Eyes,' with the wild cats and other exotic animals. I guess Phoebe and I did our bit, didn't we?" And a memorial fund in Bill Riley's honor still raises money to support the zoo that meant so much to him. As predictable as the hot, humid August weather, Bill Riley, Jr., hosts the talent show at the fair. "The continuity in our lives, Phoebe's and mine, feels good. We will never be out of touch."

Savoring Good Times
Tricia and Celeste

It's Pumpkinfest in Yaphank, New York, on Long Island. There are concerts and sheep-shearing demonstrations and kids picking out pumpkins in the fields. This has been a small but thriving community since it was founded in the mid 1700s. One of the current residents, Tricia, has been passionately involved with Yaphank's lovely old homes for years—beginning with the restoration of the gracious Hawkins-Dooley House, with its wide, welcoming porches. More recently, she has restored two houses next door to each other. One has a little retreat at the back of the property, on the water, where Tricia goes to read and rest, visited by a pair of swans that occasionally glides by. Summer guests love to spend the night here, resting in fresh linen sheets with plump old-fashioned pillows, their slips trimmed in lace. There's always a vase of freshly cut flowers, a small casual bouquet that is perfection.

Tricia is a wonder as a hostess, and her home is always open to family and friends. Astute magazine readers might recognize the small, tidy rooms with mellow pine-plank floors and tiny period windows and almost miniature fireplaces, because the historic house is often the backdrop for photography layouts. For years, Tricia has been a designer and editor—always devoted to restoration projects. On this October Sunday, she is welcoming her friend Celeste, who has baked her a ricotta pie.

As young students at St. Joseph's Academy, an all-girls Catholic high school, Tricia and Celeste often spent Sundays out of their uniforms at Celeste's home. "I am the oldest of seven kids," says Tricia, "and from a big extended family that abounds with cousins. I never lacked for kid companionship when I was growing up. But when I went to St. Joseph's, I met Celeste on the first day of school and truly had my first best friend. My wonderful family is very meat and potatoes and milk, but Celeste comes from a creative, artistic Italian family, and I loved being included in their Sunday afternoon lunches, with seven courses of delicious food. Every bite was not only digested but discussed. It might take an hour to talk about the sauce of the week." Tricia is a vegetarian, and among her favorite dishes is ricotta pie, a simple but elegant dish.

But it was more than the food, savory as it was, or even the discreet sip of Celeste's grandfather's vaunted homemade wine, that enthralled Tricia. "It was things like the after-dinner opera singing that made me think that I had died and gone to heaven. Her parents encouraged my creative talents and took me into New York City with them to go to museums and the ballet. It wasn't my family's world— they were nurses, social workers, and teachers and expected me to follow in that direction. I was so inspired by Celeste's family, because every creative effort was enjoyed and celebrated. It even influenced my college choice and curriculum. These times were life-altering for me."

Celeste found in Tricia, whom she still thinks of as "Pat," an anchor in a "world of nuns." "St. Joseph's was my parents' idea, because I was beginning to stray from my religious faith. Tricia understood my discontent and seriousness about the world, along with my sense of humor. We laughed a lot and didn't need to do much to have a good time. I guess we were lucky to live on the water and spend hours walking on the beach, talking and dreaming together. And sometimes we just hung out in our rooms."

As for those rooms, Celeste continues, "Every time I went to

Tricia's house, I could count on her having redecorated her room, using fabric to achieve a totally different look. I loved when she planned a meal for us, because she would create a charming and

Tricia (left) and Celeste during a relaxing day at the beach.

innovative table setting. These were visions of things to come in Tricia's career in home design, to be sure."

The girls shared a love of art and were in the school's art club. Celeste was amazed at her friend's superlative work. "I remember wanting her to show my parents the beautiful sepia-toned photographs of farms that she took at college. I don't think Tricia ever realized the extent and scope of her talent. My parents were so excited about the work that they encouraged her in a career in art." Celeste also enjoyed her time at Tricia's, where her grandmother was like Mary Poppins, "full of optimism, good cheer, and laughter."

"Her family always made me feel as if I were one of them. Her mom was so natural to be with, and I think she was happy that we got along so well together. She'd hang around chatting but wisely always gave us our own time."

"Now it's been a friendship of forty-four years," remarks Tricia. "A couple of years ago, I was in New York's SoHo district and did a double take when, for a moment, I thought I saw her father on the street with a film crew. It was Celeste's younger brother, Joe, a producer, who now so resembles her dad. It brought back so many memories for me. I had to think of the times when my conservative and cautious father wouldn't let me go into the city unless I went with Celeste and her family."

Celeste and her husband are both teachers, and every summer they go to Maine, where Celeste, who takes on the considerable challenges of a kindergarten class during the school year, renews her spirits gardening and painting. But it is autumn on Long Island, and everyone is back at work, except on days like this—a bright Pumpkinfest Sunday. Celeste has come to see Tricia's latest achievement—another treasured Yaphank house that has been given her magic touch, with lots of vision and dedicated hard work. "I love how genuinely passionate Tricia gets about whatever is happening in both our lives. I admire the sensitivity and empathy she has for people. You can hear it in her voice and feel it when you are with her. And of course there is the laughter that has always been a big part of our friendship—being able to see the world in many of the same ways, from way back when we met until now."

There is a freshly baked ricotta pie to slice, a walk along the water, recently read books to share, and an occasion for two old friends who might just sip a glass of wine together—a tribute to Sundays they both cherish—to relax and enjoy.

"It's like a gift in an often too busy and overcommitted life," says Tricia wistfully.

Nancy Lindemeyer

RICOTTA PIE

2 eggs

15-ounce container part-skim ricotta

½ cup grated part-skim mozzarella cheese (smoked is good, too)

¼ cup grated Parmesan cheese

¼ cup grated Romano cheese

2 tablespoons chopped fresh parsley

9-inch pie shell, prebaked for about 10 minutes

Preheat the oven to 350°F. Mix the eggs, all the cheeses, and the parsley together and pour the filling into the pie shell. Bake for about 1 hour, or until golden on top and toothpick comes out clean.

Note: You can add almost anything to this basic pie. Steamed chopped broccoli or spinach, cooked sausage, sautéed zucchini and onions, red peppers, or chopped basil are all good options. However, if adding ingredients, you will want to use a deep-dish pie shell.

To Cherish What We Have
Kat and Melanie

S ome friendships are tended like formal gardens: The plantings are in tidy rows, and one always knows what to expect, season after season. The careful gardener never forgets birthdays, and Christmas presents are in the mail to arrive the day before. And some are more like meadows filled with wildflowers strewn by Nature's unpredictable hand. Melanie and Kat tolerate a forgotten birthday and the call that never got placed during holidays because of their faith that the flame of friendship burns brightly across miles and years. "There's divinity in that," Kat says. "Since sixth grade, this sometimes tumultuous coupling has been going on for twenty years."

Russiaville (pronounced Rooshaville), Indiana, had a population of about a thousand when the girls were going to the Western School District in the midst of a "sea of corn," as Kat describes it. "It was a big deal when the school decided to pave the parking lot." It was inside this school that the two girls first met. Melanie had just had her tonsils out and couldn't really talk to the girl who sat next to her in health class. An exchange of notes began, and since then they have had plenty to talk about, including Kat's later college shenanigans.

"We were both home from college and driving down the road in nearby Kokomo when I began confessing to some freshman behavior I wasn't too proud of," she says. "Melanie didn't miss a beat, telling me all that didn't matter and she loved me just the same, for who I am.

Kat (right) and Melanie, displaying their unique senses of humor born back home in Indiana.

I think that moment provided the baseline and measurement of our friendship going forward. I never worry about telling her anything."

"Yes, Kat is still my best friend," Melanie says, "though we live apart now; she's in New York, and I'm in Indiana. At times, the distance we've lived from each other has been challenging, but we've found out that time, distance, and complicated lives haven't hurt this constant in our lives. Kat and I don't expect a lot from each other as far as the time we spend together is concerned. We just both completely cherish what we do have. It's a beautiful thing to have that sort of friendship."

Melanie continues, "Kat helped me to grow as a person. She is strong and intelligent with a zest for life that allows her to keep an open mind to possibilities. We both came from families where this was not completely understood, and she continues to inspire me to maintain the ownership of my own life and keep a positive attitude. Free advice from my New York lawyer friend!"

The good homes the girls grew up in were almost identical, which is why seeming like sisters is not difficult to comprehend. Both dads were electrical engineers, and their moms kept extremely orderly houses. To illustrate how alike their upbringing was, Melanie recalls what she said to her dad after a vacation trip she took with Kat's family: "I would have missed him, but being with Kat's dad for

Melanie (right) on a recent visit to Kat in New York.

a week was virtually the same, and if you've ever known an engineer, you know exactly what I'm talking about." Neither woman now claims to have such predictability in her own life.

"I was present at Melanie's wedding and for the birth of her two kids, Luke and Emma. Luke is precious, and I loved being around him as a baby. We had 'tummy time' together, and as I played with his toes, he giggled so adorably. And I loved watching Melanie as a mother. Once, when she was putting Luke to bed, I could hear her say, 'No, Luke, you can have only four Oreo cookies before bed—one for each year you are!' That was Melanie—only four Oreos before bed. Emma is exactly like her mother, as sweet as can be. Once, when I was babysitting the kids, Emma climbed on the kitchen island just as her parents came in the door. Since it looked like I was cooking her for dinner, I just proceeded to pretend to put her in the oven. Her husband, Joel, looked slightly horrified, but Melanie and I laughed hysterically—senses of humor born and bred in Russiaville, Indiana."

Nancy Lindemeyer

"I Miss Her"
Connie and Tracey

There are nearly 700,000 aircraft movements every day at the Dallas–Fort Worth airport. By the measure of air traffic, it is not only the busiest airport in Texas but in the United States as well—and it is the third busiest in the world. On any given day, the terminals teem with people: hustling business types pulling luggage with laptop compartments, frantic tourists making connections to nirvana vacations, college kids with weary bodies under heavy backpacks. Many are the meetings, some happy, others bittersweet.

Several years ago, Connie, her Miranda red hair remarkable even in this morass of people, kept a patient vigil, waiting for her friend Tracey. It wasn't one of their yearly Christmas reunions in Dallas. Connie had hurriedly left a work assignment in High Point, North Carolina, to meet the plane bringing home from Russia the daughter who had just lost her dad unexpectedly. Connie, whose own father died when she was in college, knew how devastated Tracey would be. "There is no way in the world I wouldn't be there for her," Connie says with the rock-solid determination that everyone who knows her understands.

"By the time I was located and able to book a flight home, my dad's funeral had already taken place," Tracey says. "Connie met me at the airport and flew with me to Texarkana and accompanied me all the way to my house. It was a surreal and kind act of friendship, and one that I will never forget."

The two women who held their arms out to each other that day first met in the junior bowling league in Texarkana. "It humbles me to remember that our friendship started while we slung eight-pound balls down an uneven alley in East Texas," says Tracey. That small city, reflecting her memories of school activities, childhood pranks, a mother's wisdom, and a family's flamboyant life, seems a long way from Times Square in New York and the skyscraper where Connie now works. As Connie walks, thinking of her childhood and Tracey, her voice drops and a bit of sadness echoes in the hushed, carpeted halls: "I miss her."

An early arena of Connie's athletic abilities was the bowling alley. Her mom, Dottie, the coach of her team, demanded that everyone be on her best behavior. But one day, a girl on the opposing team "was acting up something fierce," Connie remembers. When Coach Dottie had finally had enough she got the girl benched, even though it turned out that her dad was the owner of the bowling alley. That girl was Tracey.

"Tracey has always been the instigator in our friendship. I was the more reticent one, although my colleagues and friends now might not believe that. She got me to do things I'd never imagined I would. Sometimes we really got into trouble," Connie says.

She describes how her high school's tennis team was not enamored with the cheerleaders, who looked down on what they considered a less glamorous activity. (Tennis may be a fine sport, but in Texas football is a religion.) One Halloween, Connie, Tracey, and several of their friends and teammates found a way to get even for past slights. The football players and cheerleaders had parked their cars and boarded a bus to an away game. Armed with white paint and brushes, they began the fun of painting cars—until the police discovered them and insisted they clean up the mess. With what? The toilet tissue in the trunks of their cars, with which they had been

Nancy Lindemeyer

festooning trees! As Connie remembers it, Tracey thought up such stunts, and she, Connie, often "got left holding the bag."

Aha! But Tracey's take on their life in crime is that *Connie* was the one who devised their stunts and roped her in. "Once, at a football game, she used me as her surrogate protester. This was before Title IX, and tennis was the only girls' sport. Very little attention was given to anything but football. Connie painted a huge sign that said something like 'All other sports salute King Football.' She neglected to tell me in advance what she was doing; she just asked me to hold up the sign for her. And I was left arguing our cause to the principal and the rest of the administrative staff. I think I recall hearing booing."

> *I solemnly swear to be faithful to my bosom friend, Diana Barry, as long as the sun and the moon shall endure.*
>
> Lucy Maud Montgomery, *Anne of Green Gables*

Despite that early discipline experience with Connie's mom, Tracey learned to love the no-nonsense working woman who had to depend on her daughter to hold up her end at home. Tracey's family life was very different. While Connie was being raised by a wise mother with cautionary tales, "Tracey's dad would help you envisage how you could do something, never rejecting any idea out of hand. He made me realize that the world was my oyster and that there was opportunity out there to be grabbed and adventures to be savored. 'Why not?' was the mantra, not 'Why would you want to do that?'"

Tracey took her father's enthusiasms seriously. Connie ticks off Tracey's accomplishments: "She took French literature at the University of Texas and then studied for a year at the Sorbonne.

Along the way, she gained an advanced degree in advertising from Northwestern University and was teaching classes at Texas. She speaks French, Spanish, Italian, and some German. There's a long laundry list of her world travels. She is always pushing the envelope. And so it is probably not unexpected that she was on an adventure when her dad died."

"I miss her." Three words that evoke a world of shared experiences, from high school high jinks to being roommates during college and their early working years in New York. "Who else would go to seven movies with me in one day? We did that one Saturday in college! We still love seeing movies together, but the most amazing thing to me is that we won't see each other for months and yet we settle down without any fuss to watch a television show and just be with each other. That's what I love the most," says Connie.

Tracey also appreciates how organized Connie can be during visits—even scheduling naptime! And Connie is the most loyal of friends, perhaps to a fault. In college, a fellow classmate was terribly unkind to Tracey, who, with time, forgave her. But not Connie, at least not yet. "I will never condone what she did to my friend."

"We have remained friends precisely because we are always rooting for each other." Tracey says. "We are always looking for the best in each other and are completely ignorant of our failings. Our personalities are vastly different, but some strange glue of our childhood has held us together like virtual twins. I am so lucky to have Connie in my life—even though she still beats me at tennis! Actually, I think I am the better player, but Connie, as in all things, tries harder."

This year at Christmas, as always, the two will meet in Dallas, flying into that busy airport once more, with the joy of the season and friendship in their hearts.

Nancy Lindemeyer

Under Watchful Eyes
Judy and Retta

Judy sleeps deep in the mattress at Retta's. Lately, every couple of months, business brings her from California back to Highland Park, Illinois, near Chicago. "Sometimes I'm only here for twenty-four hours, but where else would I find the perfect guest room, great bath, and fabulous dinner?" asks Judy. Retta lives very near where the women grew up and even belongs to the same club to which Judy's parents belonged. "It's like coming home—walking in familiar steps again," says Judy.

"Our matchmaker was kindergarten," says Retta. "Judy lived right across from the school, and one of the charms of being chums was having lunch at Judy's when our famous Midwest winter weather made it tough for us little tykes to tramp home at noontime. How great the hot tomato soup and grilled-cheese sandwiches tasted on a cold snowy day! I called Judy's the 'foodie house' because her freezer was filled to the brim with things like Good Humor bars, and the coffee table had what seemed like a bottomless candy dish."

In summer, when Chicago's hot, humid weather comes in like a stalking panther (unlike the cooling fog that comes in on little cat feet), the pool at Retta's was the place to be. "In the driveway, we'd play seven-up, tossing the ball around for hours," Judy remembers. She describes herself as not very athletic or willing to take risks in those days and says, "Retta can hardly believe that now my daughter and I have run marathons and in our travels have done some pretty challenging hiking. Some things do change."

On the subject of Judy's mother, both women have vivid recollections of a larger-than-life woman who could make their young lives into an exciting adventure. "She was really eccentric in many ways. Everyone remembers that she spoke in a loud voice because she was extremely hard of hearing. In contrast, my mom was a private woman, a voracious reader, very neat and organized," Retta says, assessing a time when Judy's mom dressed flamboyantly, was effusive in everything she did, and hugged and kissed the girls often. "She'd load us in the station wagon—Judy, me, and Judy's two younger sisters—and just take us everywhere. There was always something going on in her world."

"My mother loved the visual arts, music festivals, and was a patron of dance groups," says Judy. "We all got the benefit of her interests and her energy. She was also known for her exotic collection of necklaces. Then I didn't used to understand or appreciate them, but now I definitely do. I have a wild, chunky copper chain that converts to a belt that belonged to Mom—and I wouldn't part with it for the world."

One thing that Judy's mother made very clear was her fondness for Retta. She admired her; not only was she beautiful on the outside, but also on the inside, and she was a good influence on Judy. "We were raised with the same values," says Judy, "and we knew right from wrong. Retta was so genuine, and my mother loved her as if she were in our family." The time would come when Judy's mom's illness brought Judy to Highland Park often, and Judy and Retta saw her through good days and bad. "I felt so for Judy trying to care for her mother long-distance," Retta says. Before her death, Judy's mother left very specific instructions as to the four people outside of the family she would allow at her funeral—and Retta was among them. "She was always there—she always did for us. She made such a big

Nancy Lindemeyer

impression on me, and it was an honor to me to have her regard me so highly," Retta says in tribute.

Under such watchful eyes, the girls went through all the grades together. In high school, they had different circles of friends and never any jealousy, something of which they are still fiercely proud. They did go off to the University of Michigan in Ann Arbor together and were sorority sisters until the end of their sophomore year. Then things changed dramatically. Retta got married and moved to Israel. "I was her maid of honor with a heavy heart. I thought I'd never see her again," Judy recounts, still with a sense of foreboding in her voice. But in a year, Retta and her husband returned to Highland Park, and Judy felt a huge sense of relief.

Judy finished college, where she prepared for a career as an audiologist. Having a mother with a hearing problem had inspired her to help kids who were hearing-impaired. They see each other only sporadically now, as Judy's marriage and career have taken her to Iowa and then to California, where she is now an executive in a health-care company. Both women are mothers and grandmothers— young, beautiful, and energetic ones, with interests that would have pleased Judy's mom. They have a lot to talk about in the twenty-four hour visit. And they know that Judy will find her way to that perfect guest room again soon. Somewhere, perhaps deep in an attic, is a photo of them side by side with their pledge to be friends forever inscribed on it. It would be lovely to find, they both agree; but they have all the years, all the times good and bittersweet, etched in their memories forever.

The Fourth Sister
Wendi and Debbie

"In the South," says Memphis native Wendi, "we call all our parents' friends 'aunt' and 'uncle.' But 'Aunt Mommy' was the special name Debbie and I created for our respective mothers. We were that close, and Debbie was like a fourth sister to me." Debbie, an only daughter, was happy to be included in the family, especially on Friday-night sleepovers with Wendi's grandmother's cheese spaghetti on the menu—like nothing she has eaten before or since. Whatever was in that dish has stayed in the senses of these two women for decades.

Wendi has been a very-much-in-demand art photographer in New Orleans, New York, and Denver, where she now lives. She collects antiques, much like the ones in the homes she and Debbie grew up in. Old fabrics and clothes are a special passion. Follow her around a museum collection or a show of vintage fashions and you can almost see things moving together in her mind. "Often we pitched our blanket tent over my mother's dining-room table for our elegant pretends. Once we even appropriated Aunt Phyllis's exquisite and definitely forbidden cordial glasses to take a princess's tiny libation of apple cider. Of course, we ate spaghetti there, too, like the two little miscreant kids we sometimes were," remembers Wendi.

Clothes play an important role in Wendi's first recollections of Debbie: "She had come to spend the night. I think she was about six years old, and I have a vision of her sitting on the beige sofa

Wendi's mom with "the sisters"—
Wendi (front row, right)
with Debbie (front row, left).

impeccably dressed in a skirt, with an embroidered white cardigan and shoes like white dancing slippers. She looked like she was going to a proper tea party, and from that time to this, she has always had a beautiful and unique sense of style." Wendi had a bit of a war going on with her own mother over the "scratchy" skirts and blazers that she and her sisters were compelled to wear.

Both women have a rich heritage of grandmothers and mothers who were creative and involved in the visual arts. The Aunt Mommies prowled Memphis antique shops and even took painting classes together. When Debbie and her mother ran a needlepoint shop for a time, Wendi's mom painted canvases for them.

"Wendi's talent was definitely inborn," says Debbie, who herself has a thriving jewelry design business that began with a few pieces featuring the creative use of beads. Each admires the other's achievements, but they are quick to admit that there was a time when they explored other friendships—outside the realm of the blanket tent—and sparked jealousies and hurts. "Now I can't imagine not having Debbie in my life, though we don't see each other that often. We have a bond that just can't be broken, despite those trying times, when one or the other of us felt left out." And says Debbie: "I am still friends with Wendi because she was an integral part of my childhood. What we shared then has been a great influence on who we became as women. I want to be Wendi's friend for many of the same reasons I wanted to be her friend when we were small. I honor and revere this authenticity."

The busy businesswoman, who has raised two daughters and caters to a cat named Uggie, and the artist of luscious hand-tinted photographs, who corrals a twelve-year-old skateboarder, have days of such forbidden pleasures as drinking from fragile cordial glasses to remember. And the grace and beauty of Aunt Mommies who shared their taste for lovely things enrich their lives, personally and professionally, every day.

NANA'S CHEESE SPAGHETTI

3 tablespoons olive oil

2 large onions, diced well

6 garlic cloves, minced

28-ounce can Italian-style tomatoes

15-ounce can tomato sauce

6-ounce can tomato paste

Dash of paprika

1 bay leaf

Salt and pepper to taste

16-ounce package spaghetti

Parmesan cheese, grated

Heat oil in a large saucepan. Saute onions and garlic until soft. Mash the tomatoes in the can with a fork and add to pot. Add a little water to the can and add to the mixture. Stir in tomato sauce, tomato paste, and seasonings. Bring to a boil, then reduce to a simmer and cook for about 2 hours, stirring occasionally. Remove bay leaf before serving.

Cook spaghetti following the package instructions. Drain and rinse with cold water to reduce starch and prevent sticking. Add sauce and toss. Serve with plenty of grated Parmesan cheese.

Note: This same sauce makes an excellent Shrimp Creole. Once the sauce is done, simply add raw, clean, deveined shrimp and cook until done.

Shared Memories

Who else remembers? All of us are fascinated, in one way or another, with the experience of childhood.

A small event, something that passed in an instant, is often the first memory a woman will share when asked about her first best friend. Such recollections provide valuable insights into the person we were destined to become. Without the ones who shared those small moments, in what seemed like a fleeting girlhood, think of what we would miss in the understanding and often pure enjoyment of ourselves.

And just how do we keep up with the girl who roller-skated with us for endless hours or the chums who diligently supported our dreams of the future—even when they seemed far away? Some carefully tend the friendship over the years through prescribed rituals; others take advantage of fortuitous experiences when they present themselves. No matter what way we choose, our shared memories are tenderly enfolded in the albums of our lives.

Chapter Two
Mary and Carol

A n early memory—smelling chrysanthemums, the head-clearing fragrance tickling her nose. Mary brought the bouquet home, courtesy of her new friend—a slightly older, tomboyish blond girl with a pageboy hairstyle. They lived across the street from each other in cookie-cutter split-level houses on a New Jersey cul-de-sac. Soon the girls wanted to have everything the same: clothes, bikes, shoes.

Being older, Carol seemed to have the upper hand. She was the one who got the guitar, the cool bell-bottoms, the oversized bulletin board that dominated the wall of her bedroom. The friends pretended they were the girlfriends of the boys on the cover of *Tiger Beat* magazine. Carol was an exceptional artist, even at an early age, and the girls created Wanted posters of neighbors from her perfect caricatures. They would laugh uproariously—and Mary says that Carol's laugh was not to be taken lightly. "You could hear it from the other side of the street," she recalls. "My mother used to say that when she heard my friend laughing, she'd laugh, too, even though she had no idea why."

When Mary went off to college in Manhattan, Carol would swing into the city, and there were serious visits to galleries devoted to photo-realism and abstract impressionism. Carol became more and more immersed in the art scene, and after a while they seemed not to

Mary's daughter, Anna (left), with her first best friend, Pearl.

have much to say to each other. For the next ten years or so, they exchanged lukewarm hellos through their mothers.

Then, one day, Mary was visiting her old neighborhood at Christmas and the phone rang. Mary says she fumbled answering it, and then heard that laugh. Why had she drifted away? She tried to remember, but nothing specific came to mind. Carol was home, too, and the girls got together in her old backyard. The playhouse where they used to imagine themselves as everything from astronauts to English orphans seemed tiny now. Was the site of their youthful adventures really this ordinary?

The mothers have now moved away from the childhood street, so the friends don't rely on them to keep in touch. The first time Carol visited Mary after her daughter, Elizabeth, was born, the toddler, then eleven months old, crawled up to her. "Steadying herself on my friend's legs," Mary says, "she pulled herself up and then held her arms to be picked up. I heard that laugh, and I was back in my childhood again, too."

Elizabeth's little sister, Anna, is six now, with a first best friend of her own. "As Carol was to me, Pearl is older than Anna and the leader," Mary notes. The girls met at three in preschool. Whoever got there first would wait for the other at the door of the school. Mary observes, "Seeing the other one come up the walkway was a moment of bliss. Anna insisted on wearing a particular pair of shoes because they match Pearl's. At preschool, they spent long hours in fantasy play, dress-up, and role play."

All children in those small-town, unhurried days had a vast inner life going on in the movies. Whole families attended together in the evenings, at least once a week, and children were allowed to go without a chaperone in the long summer afternoons—schoolmates with their best friends, pairs of little girls trotting on foot the short distance through the park to town under their Japanese parasols.

Eudora Welty, *One Writer's Beginnings*

Every week during the school year, they trade playdates at each other's houses, usually holing up in the bedroom for a few hours playing games with arcane rules. Costumes are always involved, as are some imaginary friends, often orphans, influenced by the musical *Annie*. Mary isn't sure the girls really know what orphans are.

Mary once asked Anna what she loves about Pearl. Her reply: "She's my friend, Mom. Can we send a note to Pearl?" Mary says, "Over the years, I've found notes in our mailbox laboriously written as Pearl struggles to master letters, asking Anna to a party of some kind—like a fairy party—games only the girls understand."

Nancy Lindemeyer

"What about the time you and Pearl sneaked away from school?" Mary asks, referring to an incident when Anna and Pearl didn't return to class after playtime and instead blended in with the bigger kids, who were sledding. Keeping her vow not to tell whose idea it was, Anna refuses to tell her mom now what both girls resisted confessing to the teacher. In the upcoming school year, the girls are going to different schools, so there won't be any more concerns over their not eating lunch because they chatted with each other instead. Mary is confident they'll maintain the friendship, but the mothers will have to be on their toes. Anna and Pearl are adept at cooking up events too elaborate for the moms to pull off. And Mary has to wonder what Anna will remember about her Pearl days—will it be a laugh, a fairy party, a backyard playhouse, a secret meeting in a bedroom? A new chapter is being written every day. Mary cannot help but think back on her own first best friendship with Carol.

The Comfort of Years
Ann and Virginia

In early December, Ann sits in her study—a charming place with a tumble of cookbooks, recipe files, and manuscript pages—and faithfully begins writing her Christmas letter. In the past few years, there has been a lot for this home economist and journalist to relate. A nice career that perked along for years has caught fire lately. She'd never be one to brag, heaven knows, but she has had interesting experiences lecturing and promoting a recent successful cookbook.

Ann comes from a Midwest background where, for generations, such letters were regarded almost as scripture. This ritual was a way for folks not only to touch base and send holiday cheer but also to reflect on times past as well as conjure hopes and dreams of the future. The tradition continues even as phone calls and emails have made at least part of their mission obsolete. For nearly half a century, Christmas letters have crisscrossed between Ann in Minnesota and Virginia, a farmer's wife, in northeast Iowa. They have faithfully chronicled things small, personal, and heartfelt—children born and growing up, their adult achievements, and, sadly as the years went on, the aging and loss of parents and old friends.

"I grew up in the little town of Strawberry Point in northeast Iowa, population one thousand in the late 1940s," says Ann. "This part of Iowa is not one's typical image of Iowa as acres and acres of prairie. Locals call it Little Switzerland because of the hilly terrain and the dairy farms that thrive here. My dad was the editor and publisher of the weekly newspaper, *The Press Journal*. When I started high school, my class jumped from about a dozen students to twenty as the country kids, as we called them, came to study, leaving their rural one-room schools."

Virginia was one of those country kids, and she stayed with her grandmother across the street from Ann's house during the week, returning to the farm on weekends. Ann was delighted because, as an only daughter and in such a small place, playmates were in short supply. "We walked to and from school every day, and I just liked her so much," Ann recalls. "Unlike me, Virginia had dark hair. Her eyes flashed, her laugh was contagious, and her smile lit up the block. I think the two of us wore out the sidewalk on our street merrily roller-skating all afternoon sometimes."

Both girls loved school and as scholars were closely matched—their hands were often waving in the air vying for the teacher's attention. Ann's dad bought a larger paper in Clarion at the end of Ann's sophomore year of high school, and the family moved. While she left Strawberry Point, she never left her friendship with Virginia.

When Virginia graduated, she married her high school sweetheart and settled down to be a farmer's wife, which was not just a role but a career. Wives are true partners in a farm's operation, as well as doing the cooking, canning, and child rearing. Because Doug was a dairy farmer, Virginia also took part in the care and feeding of the animals.

Ann went to Iowa State University, in Ames, and, on the advice of her dad, studied both home economics and journalism. Her career began in cookbooks and carried on in newspapers, making her something of a culinary celebrity. She's become a sort of food detective, searching out and restoring the food heritage of the Midwest. And that's where Virginia lends a hand, now and then.

"We both love to exchange our favorite recipes, and in my last book, *Hot Dish Heaven,* I looked to Virginia, wife, mother, grand-mother, gardener, and cook all rolled into one smiling package," Ann wrote in her introduction to the recipe for Pecan-Topped Sweet Potato Casserole, one of the mainstays of an Iowa-style company dinner. Ann also included the tale of taking her daughter Barbara to the farm when she was three. Barbara loved the piglets, but they did not match her storybook idea of the three little pigs, as the aggressive creatures pushed and shoved to get to their feeders. The city child was happier in Virginia's warm, safe kitchen.

Ann enjoys calls and emails from Virginia, but she always looks for that Christmas letter from the farm. It's a simple typewritten page—no pictures of garlands or sprigs of holly. "Here it is, December again, and time to send the annual Christmas letter," it begins. And then the country kid from Strawberry Point high school days recounts her trip to northern Mexico and tells of her plans to visit her son in London in the coming year. Grandkids are in colleges and universities—some in Iowa, some not. Then comes the part Ann loves most—the incidents on the farm. Deer hunters have camped in their yard, "Curt's family was here for Thanksgiving," and "Our summer was spent with me gardening and Doug fighting the multiflora roses in the woods as usual." What is Ann to make of the fact that red squirrels are scarce in northeast Iowa this year? Things small, personal, and heartfelt—the comforts of years and the blessings of friendship for Christmas and all the years.

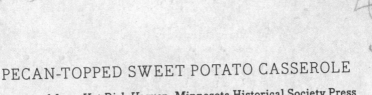

PECAN-TOPPED SWEET POTATO CASSEROLE

reprinted from *Hot Dish Heaven*, Minnesota Historical Society Press

Makes 8–10 servings

40-ounce can sweet potatoes, or 5 cups cooked
   and peeled sweet potatoes (about 4 pounds before cooking)
½ cup granulated sugar
2 eggs
⅓ cup butter, at room temperature
⅓ cup milk
1 teaspoon vanilla

Topping
¾ cup brown sugar
1 cup chopped pecans
⅓ cup flour
⅓ cup butter, melted

Preheat the oven to 350°F. Drain the sweet potatoes and mash them with the granulated sugar, eggs, butter, milk, and vanilla. Pour the mixture into a buttered 2-quart baking dish. Combine all the ingredients for the topping, then distribute it evenly over the sweet potato mixture. Bake for 35 to 40 minutes, or until a knife inserted in the center comes out clean.

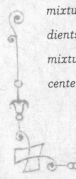

Songs in Their Hearts
Pat and the Harmonettes

The invitations for the Blues Ball are just popping up in mailboxes all over the country. It's the fifteenth anniversary of the Memphis extravaganza, and this year it will celebrate the career of Isaac Hayes, the legendary soul musician. Staged to raise funds for a variety of charities, the ball is the brainchild of Savannah, Tennessee, native Pat. She's especially proud of the funds that go to area scholarships in music. And for good reason: She herself was once a singer.

The shadows of history fall long on Savannah, where Pat's mother, Margaret, had come as a young bride to a farm that had been in her husband's family for generations. Four thousand acres of nearby fields and woods have been preserved as the Civil War battlefield where a hundred thousand troops clashed in the battle of Shiloh. Cherry Mansion, a gracious 1830s home built on Main Street as a wedding gift, was General Grant's headquarters in the spring of 1862. Growing up on the banks of the beautiful Tennessee River, Pat and her "five best friends" were very attached to their hometown— so much so that none of them has ever really left it.

"We were called the Big Six, but I don't recall who named us. It was our little private, secure domain," Pat proudly admits. "We did everything our tiny little town had to offer. We took tap dancing, ballet, and piano together as little kids and later were cheerleaders and majorettes, singing together in youth choirs at our churches." Karenina, Freeda, Wanda, Mary Ann, Jean, and Pat went through a phase when every school morning they made early phone calls to each other's homes—to the consternation of parents—to discuss in detail the uniform of the day.

Today, we talk on the phone four or five times a week, she from her sprawling country home, me from my little nest in the city. I hear her baby cry in the background; she hears me flip on my computer, or strike a match to light a cigarette. The background music we live by is utterly different; it even clashes at times. But still, when I hear her voice, when we talk about what matters in our lives, or simply make each other laugh, I think we're both moved by the same fundamental chords. They're old and familiar and deeply reassuring: the chords of shared history, scoring a waltz of closeness.

Caroline Knapp, "On Being a Twin"

The girls started a singing group known as the Harmonettes; they wore mouton coats and penny loafers and had identical haircuts. "We were invited to leave our Sunday morning radio appearances after once getting so tickled at each other's giggles we couldn't sing! Just thinking about that hilarious moment makes my heart smile. I think we giggled our way through life in those days," confesses Pat. But, she continues, "looking back, these early relationships were a precious gift. The lessons taught us early on that our formidable minds were invaluable. We learned from each other the value of loyalty, honesty, and a secure, safe refuge. We also learned that a caring friend is one you can unconditionally count on, especially when learning how to deal with jealousy and envy."

The Big Six are all still in Tennessee, and no one has moved very far from Savannah. Several years ago, all were home for the holidays, and Pat invited them to her family's farm for a reunion. There was giggling and reminiscing, but not singing—the last time they sang together was in high school. "I have never missed spending Christmas here, nor has anyone in my family, even though Mom and Dad are now gone," says Pat.

All the morning discussions about clothes—did they lead to Pat's international bridal and formal gown business and her incredible collection of lace and historical clothing? All the group singing and shared activities—did they play a part in her civic interest in founding the Blues Ball and the Jingle Bell Ball for Memphis children at the holidays? "In high school, we were involved in everything, and each of us has continued to have positive and meaningful impacts on our communities. I am equally proud of them today as I was when we excelled as teenagers. Our little hometown, Savannah, is indeed unique," muses Pat. Six girlhood friends, now in different walks of life, are still under the spell of the lovely shadows of time and place.

Keeping On Keeping On
A Dozen First Best Friends

For many girls, scouting begins at age six. They do things like march in a Memorial Day parade and make s'mores over a campfire. Friendship, fun, and a sense of community participation are goals for these first- and second-graders.

When Tammy's daughter Dylan started out as a Brownie in 1986, she had no idea that it was going to become so important to both of them. Dylan is now twenty-six and has just been married. Among those invited to the wedding: her eleven former Brownie pals and their moms.

"The girls and their moms, who all took turns being leaders, went all the way through the scouting program, and while the scouts piled up the requisite merit badges, it was never about that for them," says Tammy. "It was the service work that culminated with the Gold Award that kept the girls interested and motivated." Dylan's project was creating a one-mile nature trail at a wildlife sanctuary where injured animals are nursed back to health. "She had to decide what she wanted along the way, like having a series of bird feeders, and then organize the volunteers to get the work done," reports Tammy.

The Girl Scouts of America organization did its job well for these high-schoolers, who ended up with an impressive record of accomplishments. But the group was not about to let their friendships drift away when the girls outgrew scouting, and so Troop 440 and their mom leaders transitioned into the Best Friends Club, meeting every month to spend time together and to continue their commitments to helping others.

"We were still the leaders at the beginning, but as time went on, we saw some of our girls begin to take over, and we enjoyed watching how their leadership has grown and developed. Of course, some of the daughters have moved away and can't come to the meetings or always participate in projects. But every month, whoever can make it shows up. It's a connection we don't want to break," says Tammy.

This holiday season, the club will continue its tradition of adopting two families. They prepare complete meals and buy gifts from the children's wish lists. "At Christmastime, we go to lunch and have a wrapping party. We like to have fun and enjoy one another, too. That's always been part of the mix. Once we rented a big house and had a giant slumber party with everybody sharing the responsibilities of cooking and entertaining," Tammy remembers with such pleasure. The club also helps each other out. For one member, there was a complete wedding put on for her son, from baking the cake to taking photographs to decorating the hall; for another, a twenty-fifth anniversary renewal of wedding vows; and for several, help at times of family problems or illness.

It seems almost unimaginable to Tammy and the other mothers that there are now grandmothers amongst them. Two of the girls have baby daughters, and there's a little boy on the horizon (he has mascot duties waiting for him). Girl Scouting was set up to make good citizens of little girls and young women. With Troop 440, the mission was accomplished, and there's a long tradition of friendship that just may never end.

Nancy Lindemeyer

There for Suzy

Suzanne and Carol

Minnesota's Edina High School has a record to be proud of: It is always on the list of the best one hundred high schools in the country. Over the years it has produced a distinguished group of alumni as well and, several years ago, inaugurated its Alumni Hall of Fame. There is an induction ceremony, and then plaques are placed in the school's new wing so that students can appreciate the impact that those who have gone before them have had in the world—achievements that they can aspire to emulate.

When Carol received an invitation to attend the event that would honor Suzanne, Class of 1970, she was thrilled, not only for her friend to receive such recognition but because it was a rare chance to see this incredibly busy woman. "From the time she was five, Suzy, as we still affectionately call her, wanted to be a doctor; we always knew that," Carol says. The "we" includes the third girl in their trio, Lynn, whom Suzy also asked to sit at her table. The three went all through middle and high school together.

On the day of the induction, several other distinguished physicians, a noted children's book author, and the first lady of Minnesota were feted. Suzy was indeed in good company, and she looked lovely, her soft shoulder-length hair reminiscent of the style she wore as a teenager when the three girls traveled to California together. On one lapel was the flower of the night; on the other, her signature cameo, bequeathed to her by her dad's mother, a hardworking and independent woman who was a professional photographer in North Dakota and Minnesota.

My dear friend Millie, now a widow like myself, occasionally comes to stay when up in town for shopping. Some parts of the past have not quite lost their sweetness, or so I think when we both rejoice in each other's company. Looking at her is like looking at a mirror image of myself. We always hearten each other, indulge in little extravagances, laugh at our vanity. For it survives!

Anita Brookner, *Brief Lives*

"I was an only child, and Carol and Lynn were like adopted sisters to me. Even though we have not had continuous contact, I have always remembered how they encouraged me to go to medical school, even when a high school counselor tried to persuade me to follow my mother and grandmother into nursing," says a humble Suzanne—the name by which she is now known to colleagues and doctors and researchers around the world. Suzy's friends spent lots of time at her home when they were growing up, and there were the requisite hours on the telephone between the serious studies in science class for her. But it was their California trip—right after they graduated from high

Nancy Lindemeyer

school—that all three women recall as a highlight.

The new grads were treated to a visit to Suzy's Aunt Shirley, who was the personal secretary of singer and television personality Dinah Shore. Carol remembers, "We were from the Midwest and were so impressed with Shirley's lovely home in a suburb of Los Angeles. She was to be our parent, but while she watched out for us, she also gave us considerable freedom. Of course, we got to visit Dinah's home (and even peek in her closets!) and spend the Fourth of July at her beach house. Years later, Suzy helped me connect with Aunt Shirley when I took my family—including my mom, in her eighties, my niece, and her teenage friends—to California. We all had lunch and talked about those good old days."

After finishing her sophomore year of college, Suzy married her fiancé, David, in his hometown of Hood River, Oregon. It was a hike from Minnesota, but Carol and Snook, another member of the gang who used to hang out in Suzy's family room feasting on her mom's pizza, were Suzy's attendants. "It was such a wonderful time. The ceremony was so lovely and intimate. And the next day, Suzy, David, one of David's attendants, and I took a trip along the Hood River," Carol remembers fondly.

"I always admired Suzy, who knew exactly what she wanted to do in her career," says Carol, who became a psychologist after flirting with journalism at college. Suzy's personal and professional life became jam-packed during the next twenty years. In 1978 she graduated from the Mayo Clinic School of Medicine. (She had followed in her grandmother's steps to Mayo, but as a medical student rather than a nurse.) Carol reels off her friend's résumé with a great sense of pride: a residency in surgery at Massachusetts General Hospital; a medical staff fellowship at the National Institutes of Health; a position on the faculty of the department of surgery at the University of Pittsburgh, where her specialty was pediatric transplant surgery. Today, Suzanne is one of only two women in the country with her own research institute, and she is world renowned for her discoveries in the field of immunology and cellular therapeutics. She is also the mother of two grown children, whom her nurse mother helped raise so Suzy could follow her destiny.

The reunion at Edina High has now led to getting together far more often. Carol is still in the Minneapolis area and sees Suzy when she comes to the Mayo Clinic for meetings of a board she is on. Lynn sometimes is able to be there on family business, so the three can relax and have dinner together. "Last year when Suzy and Lynn were both back and learned that Mother had fallen and broken her arm, these two insisted, 'Let's go visit your mom.' You can think of many things to do with precious time other than visit a ninety-two-year-old in a transitional care unit. But they wanted to."

When Carol was recently diagnosed with breast cancer, she found out what truly good friends she had in Lynn and Suzy. "During my recovery, Lynn was with me for six weeks, amazing and miraculous. And Suzy was there to problem-solve for me as to what options were open to me and where I should receive care. It was incredible to have a gifted physician as my advocate. I could hardly believe how tremendously compassionate she was. Care, knowledge, information, and friendship—I was especially blessed."

One of the silly things that comes to mind as Carol remembers their growing up is the many times a bunch of girls would go to the shopping center and chip in for a series of photos at the photo booth. "Of course this required precision timing, and we weren't always on the mark. Sometimes we'd have a photo of the curtain over someone's head." If these girlhood images survive, they may be of interest to more than the Edina kids in the shots. Suzanne has more than once been mentioned as a candidate for a Nobel Prize. In her unassuming way, the modest but determined doctor once said of such speculation, "We do our work." One suspects that, if that time comes, Lynn and Carol will be in Stockholm to cheer her on.

Nancy Lindemeyer

Junk Food Heaven

Forget Tolstoy
and his happy families.
We all know a household
is defined by its snack food.
Chips or pretzels?
Soda or apple juice?
This was what made us.
The healthy house
had oppressive standards
(nothing more decadent than a raisin),
another had peculiar rules
(like that ban on anything darker than beige).
Then there was the kitchen
that was a Reddi-wip-coated,
barbecue flavored,
chocolate-chipped,
marshmallow-filled,
Cheez-Whiz-covered dream.
We luxuriated in each other's snack foods,
stepping into another world with our mouths.
Our friend's world,
her mom's world,
but best of all, not our world—
at least for a few hours.
A trip to another planet
in the kitchen across the street.

—Robin Reiser

Gentle Lessons

Oh, what little blackboards children can be. First impressions, some as delicate as a flower pressed in a book, can have lasting consequences. Things we learn at home—through "little, nameless, unremembered acts of kindness and of love"—have far-reaching effects in our lives. First best friends and their families, especially their moms, are life heroines.

This section features several incomparable stories of the wisdom and goodness of the mother next door. What was shared by little girls was more than dolls and afternoons spent on swing sets. They shared homes, too, and these sometimes became havens from the distresses of their own homes. Admiration for the first best friend who invited them over after school flowed to the mother who was there, with her quiet charm and gentleness. The first best friend who thrived in security and comfort shared it with her chum. It was nothing premeditated, just an act of girlhood generosity hardly noticed at the time.

Look, too, for mothers who sewed with such beauty that the loss of their efforts taught a daughter what to appreciate in life—and what is truly precious. And look to a daughter who brought two first best friends together again when she was born and shared her own wonder as she grew to womanhood. Home schools are the scenes of gentle lessons that last a lifetime.

Lasting Impressions
Bernadette and JoAnn

"She taught me how to clean a bathroom—a pretty practical lesson," says Bernadette of the little friend she made at four. Bernadette doesn't remember moving into the apartment building in Suitland, Maryland, but there was JoAnn across the hall with her parents and a brother and a sister. An only child, Bernadette was anxious for companionship, and JoAnn was looking for a refuge from her more hectic home. "We were constantly together and underfoot. JoAnn wouldn't even stay away when I had chicken pox—poor thing got even sicker than I was."

JoAnn, as one of three children, was expected to help with chores. Bernadette's mother was a practical woman, as she herself was raised in a large family in Tennessee, and made her child understand that the two of them were in it together—"Hon, I am going to need your help"—when tragic circumstances left the two of them alone. "It was more than just helping out around the house, it was being partners in our lives. That spirit of cooperation always made the difference for me," Bernadette says.

"Her mother never raised her voice to Bernadette," JoAnn, now a grandmother, recalls. "Even as a little girl, I admired this comely woman so much. Bernadette was lovely and well behaved and always beautifully dressed, despite the fact that money was not plentiful in those postwar days." Bernadette smiles when she

Nancy Lindemeyer

As the shutter clicks, JoAnn (left) slips her arm around Bernadette.

remembers her mother using bottle after bottle of starch to make her school clothes as perfect as possible. "Of course, I came home looking like a wreck, to Mother's consternation. Nevertheless she didn't give up. She would get up early to go to the sales to make sure that she was on hand to get the best buy in a winter coat, for example. If we were in it together, she more than did her part to make my life as pleasant and normal as possible."

Looking back, both women turn their attention and affection to a mother who was a strong teacher of common sense and decency. "Mother had an uncanny ability to read people," Bernadette recalls, "and she never missed an opportunity to point things out to us. If a kid was acting up in a store, she'd be pretty clear that JoAnn and I were not to fall into that kind of unacceptable behavior. Once she got after us for giggling about a girl in our class who came to school with her lunch in a bread wrapper, rather than in the nice folded wax paper our mothers protected our sandwiches in. Mother had come from poor circumstances and would not abide such unkind behavior. JoAnn got it, just as I did. I know it left a lasting impression."

"Bernadette's mother has been my role model in raising my own three daughters," JoAnn confirms. "She had a natural eloquence and was sincere and truly remarkable—the driving, steadying force in my life when I needed one."

Like many a pair of first best friends, these girls were physical opposites. JoAnn is still tiny; Bernadette is a tall, striking woman, who has always worn her height with pride. Her mother insisted on it. Holding your head up, even at the top of a frame larger than that of any other girl in the class, was part of the creed that came from her fierce Scotch-Irish kin. One day the girls were playing hide and seek at Bernadette's. It was a small place, and Bernadette could not imagine why she could not find her friend. Then she spotted wee toes sticking out—

Bernadette (left) and JoAnn on May Day.

from where? "My mother was at her familiar stand—the ironing board—wearing her long housecoat. Those tiny, tiny toes were just visible poking out from beneath the skirt! I'll never forget how frustrated I was until I found her. And to think she was a year older than I and so very delicate." There is hearty laughter in her voice remembering something from so long ago as if it were yesterday.

JoAnn remembers what a haven Bernadette's home was for her, a place her mother made calm and secure. "At one point Bernadette moved upstairs, very long stairs. I managed to get up without any trouble but was always falling on my way down. I guess they were too much for my little legs. But no matter. I never seemed to get hurt, just shaken up a bit. My tumbling really worried Bernadette," JoAnn says with a tickle in her voice.

Family photos show the girls dressed identically for a school May Day celebration with crepe-paper ribbons in matching colors that Bernadette's mother made for their hair. "We loved making May baskets and hanging them on doorknobs," says Bernadette, now a freelance writer who lives in an apartment in downtown Minneapolis. She's the kind of neighbor who hands out party invitations as freely as she used to hand out May flowers. Her cheerful home has a wonder-

Nancy Lindemeyer

Bernadette (far left) on her birthday with JoAnn, her brother, and some neighborhood lads.

ful collection of photographs of her mother's family, including her grannies wearing their characteristic bonnets.

After JoAnn's family moved, when she was about twelve, their coveted togetherness ceased for a time. The mothers kept in touch, especially at Christmas, and there were even a few family visits when they were adults. Over the last decade, however, Bernadette and JoAnn have truly restored their friendship, and JoAnn is planning a trip to Minneapolis—"but not in the winter," Bernadette advises her friend, who lives in a more temperate climate in North Carolina. Stash, the big black-and-white cat, will be on hand to curl up on a lap or pose regally on a dresser top, and a host of Bernadette's friends and neighbors will make their way to apartment 8B to celebrate the reunion.

"I think of Bernadette so often. Sometimes when I see on TV that there is snow in Minneapolis, I'll give her a call and ask her to describe the snow to me, and we both think back to being packed tight into snowsuits and allowed to go out and play, throwing snowballs and making snowmen. It brings back a warm memory. Just hearing her voice, calm and kind, like her mother's, is a balm. I'd love to see the twinkling lights she has on her balcony covered in a frosty white."

"We've been part of each other's life in a way that can't be broken," says Bernadette. "After all, she is one of the few people left who remembers my dad when he was young and handsome—the tall man across the hall." And on a lighter note: "I saw my first television show at JoAnn's—Milton Berle. I'm not about to forget that!"

She was a year or so older than I—that is, about eight —and her five or six brothers, I supposed in their teens, seemed like grown men to me. But Gwendolyn and I, although we didn't see each other very often, were friends, and to me she stood for every thing that the slightly repellent but fascinating words "little girl" should mean. In the first place, her beautiful name. Its dactyl trisyllables could have gone on forever as far as I was concerned. . . . She would arrive carrying a doll or some other toy; her mother would bring a cake or a jar of preserves for my grandmother. Then I would have the opportunity of show- ing her all my possessions all over again.

Elizabeth Bishop, "Gwendolyn"

Nancy Lindemeyer

Weathering Ill Winds
Anna and Mary

"She is my history," says Anna in her matter-of-fact Queens, New York, sort of way. "We never let each other forget where we came from." Anna isn't referring only to their backgrounds as the kids of Irish immigrants in an enclave of many first-generation offspring, a bridge or subway ride from Manhattan. Where they come from is a place in the heart.

When Anna finished her sixth-grade year, her mom became ill, and the slight, shy girl with the almond-shaped eyes was sent to live with her warmhearted Aunt Phyllis. Anna was to learn the true meaning of the old spiritual, "Sometimes I Feel Like a Motherless Child." She felt plaintively alone as the lyrics describe: "Motherless children have a real hard time." Missing her old school friends, she was in no frame of mind to recruit new ones at St. Kevin's, a few steps from her new home. Her spirits were very low without the life her child's heart had believed would never change.

Always an achiever, Anna decided to take the test for the college preparatory curriculum at St. Francis High School. On that Saturday, she spotted a girl she had seen at St. Kevin's. "It was not an immediate attachment, but over the new school year at St. Francis, we steadily grew closer," says Anna, who still describes herself as being a deliberative sort who does not rush into things.

"When we were fourteen," Mary recounts, "Anna was at my

house and we were planning to go to a church fair. It was something really special for us because it was the first time we were going to be allowed to go out alone at night. About four o'clock, Aunt Phyllis called and asked that Anna come home immediately. We were really disappointed! Outraged, in fact, the way only teenagers can be, because we thought Anna's family had thought better of our outing. It was later that evening that I found out that Anna's mother, who had been ill for so long, had died. From then on, Anna spent a lot of time with my family."

Lately, Aunt Phyllis has been visiting Mary's mother, who is now in a nearby nursing home, every couple of weeks. Neither she nor Anna has ever forgotten how Mary's family helped to fill a void in Anna's life. The girls' attachment had also easily spilled over to the two older women. All these years later, Anna thinks about coming to Mary's after school for mom food—such stick-to-the-ribs fare as chicken à la king or chicken salad—that had to be made with both white and dark meat and never any mayonnaise other than Hellmann's. (Note: While the chicken salad was made from scratch, Mary confesses that her mother opened a can for chicken à la king. Anna didn't recall that.)

Most important, however, is that a motherless girl found a model for her own future role as the mother of two enchanting grammar-school girls, Katie and Emma. Anna says what she most liked about Mary's mom was her gentleness and calming presence that made home a place of safety and security. And she appreciated the joy of having young girls in the house. Both girls adored playing with Mary's dollhouse, which was really the stage for her collection of miniatures. "It wasn't really the type of house we kids should have been touching, but we did. I can't imagine girls of this age now being so enchanted with a dollhouse. As I look back, I think it was because neither of us lived in what we thought of as a real house. I lived in an apartment and Anna in an attached house, and we hoped for a time when we would have homes of our own."

Nancy Lindemeyer

Mary's mother and Aunt Phyllis stayed constant even when the girls had fallings-out—the entire junior year of high school went by without the two uttering a word to each other. After high school, there was another bumpy patch for Mary. Both girls had their hearts set on attending the same college to study graphic design, but Anna was accepted and Mary wasn't. "At the time, I was devastated as I watched Anna begin to live out my dream of being a designer. But as it turned out, I ended up writing and working my way up in publishing and advertising from copywriting to marketing director. Anna and I occasionally now work on freelance projects together—I write and she designs. Who would have predicted that?"

I met her twenty-two years ago at a writers' lunch and a remarkably soulful friendship was born. Over the years we've worked, laughed, cried, dreamed, and shopped together. And on occasion, been Lucy and Ethel together.

Sue Monk Kidd

Anna was pleased when she and Mary ended up working in the same company before they were married and had children. There were times when they got together that they inevitably revisited the high school prom when they double dated. And they savored such memories as the incredible toasted bagels, generously buttered, they ate with relish at the diner where they stopped after school to reassess the events of the day. When that wasn't enough, there were phone calls after dinner, a ritual so many school friends followed in those pre-Internet days. Now, as work friends, they discussed their aspirations and the events of rapidly changing lives as careers blossomed and families began.

Both women were married in the same church; their eldest daughters were born eight weeks apart and were christened at the same church service. While the relationship has had its ebb and flow, and months have passed without a call or a visit, they are now in constant communication. "I'm just calling to check in," Anna says, as she begins the weekly conversation. "The lovely thing about the balance of good and not-such-terrific times is that it reminds me that friendships can weather some ill winds—life is like that," affirms Anna, with the wisdom of a woman who truly knows what those words mean.

Mary says that it must be the Irish in her, but some of the most poignant milestones in their relationship have been surrounded by loss. "I was with Anna when her mother passed away. And when my father died, Anna was there for me. His funeral was at nine o'clock the morning of 9/11. I had no idea of the turmoil that was going on in the world outside, although I did see the smoke on the Manhattan skyline. The talk of a plane crash did not register with me. As I walked behind my father's casket, I was aware that the church was almost empty. My heart sank, because I couldn't imagine why. When the priest began the service by praying for the victims of the World Trade Center, I realized that there were reasons for the low attendance—many were turned back on the roads, I understand, but, miraculously, not Anna nor dear Aunt Phyllis. I'll never forget seeing them there. My heart swelled."

And somehow the tables got turned on the generations, as Mary credits Anna's model of motherhood—being at home with her kids and managing to work freelance—as her inspiration to do the same. Once they moved delicate figures cautiously around make-believe dollhouse rooms with dreams of having homes of their own. Today, they manage busy, productive, fulfilling lives with the pleasure of an old friend's call—"just checking in."

Nancy Lindemeyer

The Three of Us
Jen and Barbara Lynn

"I put a spell on you," Jen sings, belting out this rock classic along with Screamin' Jay Hawkins while putting on her mascara.

"From the beginning, we talked a lot about music," says Barbara Lynn, as she brings back this perfect mental snapshot of her past with Jen. "We still do." Food, too, is an important touchstone for two women who once tried to eat their way across New York City, by following a local guidebook's recommendations.

"We met on Long Island one summer when Jen, who was from Houston, was a nanny for several of her young cousins and I was home from school. One of the favorite things we did that summer was to drive to Montauk to admire the cute Irish boys who came over for jobs at the beach communities. We'd listen to music on the radio and drink very strong coffee." It was the first time that Barbara Lynn had a friend with whom she felt she could just be herself. "We matched wits, we matched clothes, and we matched wicked jokes with each other." Perhaps hearkening back to their first summer together, Jen says, "We swim in the same water." Barbara Lynn viewed Jen as the stronger swimmer, who inspired her to go further and be more fearless. And now there is another fish in their pond, Jen's teenage daughter, Zoë, Barbara Lynn's goddaughter.

Living together in London as poor students had not worked out well for Jen and Barbara Lynn. Jen went first, pursuing her art degree. Barbara Lynn followed in her own academic pursuits. "There was no sunshine *ever* and horrible food," Jen says, blaming the climate and the cuisine for their falling out. Unfortunately, years went by without contact. In the meantime, both finished college. Jen married an Englishman, and they settled in Spain. When Barbara Lynn heard from her mom that Jen was pregnant, things changed dramatically.

"I just knew I had to talk to her," says Barbara Lynn. "I called international directory assistance and had an operator in Malaga, Spain, contact every number associated with their name. It must have cost me fifty dollars, which was a lot for me at the time. I finally reached her, and it was like nothing ill had ever happened between us. And from the time Zoë was born, we have been bound together as never before."

The bond was strengthened by Jen and Zoë's return to the States. "My goddaughter has just turned fourteen," Barbara Lynn says with fierce pride. "She's a student at Cab Calloway School for the Performing Arts, a budding actress. When I visited Zoë and Jen at their home in Delaware recently, we looked at the birthday videos on Zoë's digital camera. It was a revelation: Zoë and her friends were singing karaoke just like Jen and I used to; the boys had floppy haircuts and torn jeans— the girls in motion were a montage of swirling earrings and striped shirts. It seemed to me that Zoë was the star in this crowd. Maybe she was truly just another awkward teenager, but, watching her, a member of a new generation, hum Beatles' tunes, I couldn't help but see something exceptional—the best of my first best friend."

"It began on Long Island one summer, this sojourn across continents," says Jen. "We've shared so much—good times, joblessness, home purchases, you name it. I adore her family—her parents and brother and his wife and children. Her husband is teaching my daughter to drive! We might take for granted the laughs and hand-holding through life's miseries, but never our Zoë." Love has endured, grown, and now has a bright star to help guide and light the future.

Nancy Lindemeyer

Being Strong for Each Other
Bethany and Crystal

B ethany is an aspiring blues singer. It might be difficult to understand how a young woman of twenty-five could have had the life
experience required to make music that goes deep into the soul. But
Crystal, her friend from age five, knows that Bethany's latest lyrics
are a poignant recitation. "Take place where you belong. / Time after
time / I'll feel wrong. / Just dance, lady, dance." At her last show,
Bethany dedicated this song to Crystal, the little girl she met at
church in Modesto, California.

Church became a place where the girls flourished, and they did
not at first recognize the differences in their families and their ways
of life. Bethany's mom had even dated Crystal's dad in college, so
they seemed quite similar. They were just happy kids who had fun at
Sunday school gatherings, and Bethany felt welcome and safe visiting Crystal's lovely home. "I loved the room with the grand piano,"
says the future musician. Bethany began to spend more and more
time at her friend's, and when her parents went through a difficult
divorce, she and her sister lived with Crystal's family for a time.

Both women recall the night that Bethany and her sister came to
stay. "I was so upset, but Crystal's mom made it seem like we were
camping and let us have pizza on a Tuesday night—a real and unusual treat. Crystal and I stayed up late, and she let me talk about

Bethany and Crystal (left) at a gathering after church.

anything I needed to. She did ask that I not move the Bible from her bedside, unless I wanted to read it. Then we read verses together that were comforting to me. This was a pattern I was to enjoy many times since. Crystal takes time out of her life to make sure that I am okay." Crystal's memory: "It was one of those childhood moments that makes you realize that something exists outside of yourself, and I remember thinking that Bethany was the strongest person I knew."

As compelling and binding as these events were at the time—and would be again later on—high school was not a good time for this relationship. "We never have had a fight, even then, but I have to confess to being envious of Crystal, who could do all the things like school and church trips. My mother just didn't have the resources. And here I was, a chubby kid unsure about myself, and Crystal was thin and so privileged."

"I'd keep dancin', / Spirit invokes me so"—Bethany's lyrics express how her life was propelling her toward a musical career. She moved to San Francisco, and Crystal once traveled from Los Angeles, where she was in college, to see Bethany perform.

But mostly the women left it to their mothers to pass on news of each other. Then they discovered that they were both in New York, had moved there within six months of each other. As is so often the

Nancy Lindemeyer

case, life in the big city was a great equalizer for the young women. It brought them back together. Until recently, they both had part-time jobs in the same downtown restaurant in the city. Working the Saturday-night shift allowed them to stay close despite hectic schedules—Bethany performing and Crystal studying for a master's degree in social work.

And so, on a night in the Big Apple, Bethany is behind the mike, taking center stage, while her friend is in the appreciative audience. Crystal confirms, "We're family"—which speaks volumes about the love and acceptance they are pledged to continue. "Dance, lady, dance."

What are friends for, my mother asks.
A duty undone, visit missed,
casserole unbaked for sick Jane.
Someone has just made her bitter.

Nothing. They are for nothing, friends,
I think. All they do in the end
they touch you. They fill you like music.

Rosellen Brown

Dressing Dolls
Karen and Laurie-Anne

"Where are the children?" the French writer Colette remembers her mother, Sido, calling out at the end of the day to summon her young ones home. If the evening was cool, she would be wrapped in a beautiful shawl, one that Colette eventually inherited. A shawl? She had no use for it. But as a newly married young homemaker, she did want pillows—and so she cut it up to make them. Years later, she wrote how foolish she was. How she would have loved to have the garment that so warmed her precious mother to comfort her own later years. How many of us have such a lament over a lost treasure, even a small one? Today, Karen recalls hers with affection and a bit of sadness.

Karen and Laurie-Anne lived only four doors apart in their suburban Maryland neighborhood. At four, they became "fast pals," as Karen describes it. Playing with Shirley Temple dolls was one of their favorite things to do, and both of their moms used the opportunity to teach the girls to sew by making clothes and other accessories for doll play. "My mother was a brilliant seamstress," says Karen, "and she guided us to make darling little bathrobes and pretty dresses. Laurie-Anne's mother was less nimble, but she helped us make little things like towels and hankies. Oh, I wish I had those now."

Fabric, fashion, and style are still passions of Karen's. She works as an editor of a magazine for a large supermarket chain in Rochester,

Nancy Lindemeyer

The girls who wanted to be twins—Karen (left) and Laurie-Anne.

New York, and a few months ago was sent to study the tea traditions of Japan. To her friends, Karen described in meticulous detail the outfit her Japanese guide wore—the colors, embroidery, and every aspect of the design. Those early stitching lessons clearly stuck with her.

As the girls grew, Karen says they "stumbled upon an amazing fact—that we were identical twin sisters separated at birth. It was obvious to us. After all, we were both adopted and lived so close to each other. Never mind that Laurie-Anne had blond ringlets, a rosy cherubic face with bright blue eyes, and a dainty, dimpled smile, while I more resembled nineteenth-century Ellis Island photographs of babushka'd immigrant girls. Long-limbed, long-nosed, long-faced, I had wide-set olive-green eyes and a full-lipped, pie-eating grin. And I was at least four inches taller than my twin."

These dramatic differences did not shake the girls' theory nor deter them from acting on what they believed. Karen relates, "Since so many movie twins could fool even family members, it should be a cinch for us to trick our first-grade teachers. We made a plan to meet in the girls' room and switch our clothes. We giggled as we swapped outfits (how her dress covered my knees, I'm still not sure). They would *never* be able to tell which of us was which. We went back to each other's classrooms and took our twin's seat, smug in the knowledge we would never be discovered. In a few minutes, we were marched out to the hallway by our laughing teachers and propelled into our proper classrooms. It was baffling! How on earth did they tell us apart?"

Laurie-Anne and Karen, "the Mutt and Jeff" twins, as Karen's dad called them (he excelled at sarcasm, calling the lazy cat Flash), were separated when Karen's family moved to another part of Maryland. "Perhaps, like many youthful friendships, this one had that mysterious expiration date." What never expired is the memory of two adopted girls finding a family in the vivid imaginations of childhood innocence. And those darling hankies, towels, and bathrobes made for dolls—they are reminders of a happy childhood endeavor, even if they no longer exist. Colette never forgot the shawl and what it meant to her. Karen will always wish she still had her doll things—but, too, will always remember the skills she learned and exult in a well-made garment, wherever in the world she finds it.

Nancy Lindemeyer

A Doll's Life

Nylon hair,

permanent bed-head.

Stiff pink suits with silver thread.

We played.

We fought.

We did serious negotiations

over Barbie,

delighted in plastic bazooms,

explored high-heeled mules and boas,

worked out our issues with Ken.

Was she bad for our body image?

Did she make us shallow?

Did she expose us to too much pleather?

Who knows?

But armless

and muddy,

she suffered for us

while cementing about a billion bonds

between friends.

—Robin Reiser

Paths

Not all first best friends are destined to travel along together. Some do, in a more casual way, giving a nod to that girl who pops instantly into focus when asked, "Who was your first best friend?" And then, "What did she mean to you?" The answers to these questions reveal that friendship can be fragile or, perhaps more accurately, can have its time, place, and purpose.

More often than not, there are no hard feelings or defining moments when friends diverge—just forking paths that take friends who were once inseparable to new places. The journey simply wasn't made for two, as the stories in this section reveal.

For a time, though, it seemed like the closeness would never end—and life seemed unimaginable without the other. They went to camp together, lived on the same street, or struggled through college sweethearts with the same anxiety. Regardless of what followed, this still was a time in life that only the two of them shared. It may be fortunate, or call it prudent, that some of these relationships are not the stuff of lifetime devotion. But they can be appreciated for what they were, and the role they played when the shoe sizes and waist measurements were smaller, before moves across country or across town, and before families of one's own became paramount.

For those who see such friends at reunions or the grocery store, there are moments of uniqueness just the same. For some, there may be a reconverging of paths sometime in the future. One never knows when the phone will ring or an email pop up in an inbox. Paths are just that—not necessarily dead ends. Should they be, there will always be the time to remember well when the footsteps of the first best friends were on the same walk home.

A Secret Garden
Jackie and Alyssa

In her mesmerizing autobiographical tale "Julia," Lillian Hellman tells how two girls who inhabited different universes are drawn closely together. One New Year's Eve she was invited to Julia's grandparents' Fifth Avenue mansion, where the walls were covered with artwork and tables held objects she had never seen before. "Julia and I were both twelve years old that New Year's night, sitting at a late dinner, with courses of fish and meats, and sherbets. . . . Each New Year's Eve of my life has brought back the memory of that night."

When Jackie, a sheltered English girl, moved to Manhattan from London, she was as enchanted and mystified with her new world as Lillian was in Julia's family mansion. Jackie's family was very proper, "very uptight British," she confesses, as she sits in a New York restaurant with cracked mirrored walls reflecting bits and pieces of the staccato life that is the rhythm of this city. "To me, at seven, everything about America was magnificent." She flashes a smile and pushes back her glasses, a gesture that almost makes one think she wants to bring that time back into clearer focus.

Jackie's dad had received a well-deserved promotion from his company, bringing him to a new assignment in New York. "We were all so proud of him, so we arrived on wings of optimism and enthusiasm."

Nancy Lindemeyer

Smiles from ear to ear on a fancy, grown-up dinner out for Jackie (right) and Alyssa.

Jackie and her parents and younger sister settled in a very nice building, but she is quick to add that her family paid a modest rent for an apartment on the fifth floor, at the back, without any real views. On the twenty-ninth floor resided Alyssa—almost like a princess in the tower. Her dad's apartment had space and views obviously commensurate with much higher rent.

This was the first time that Jackie had met anyone whose parents were divorced. It seemed unsettling to her at first, but soon, seamlessly, Jackie was fitting into the rhythm of Alyssa's life, at school, in the third grade, and then after school at Alyssa's mother's nearby apartment, also an elegant abode, and on weekends with her dad, when the sky was almost the limit. In both places, the girls were allowed to languish on the "big people's" beds, plumped-up pillows behind them, to watch television. No such thing was allowed in Jackie's home, where rules for children were many and firm. "My own kids get to romp on my bed—I loved having that freedom, and I am happy to pass that on to them," says the mother of two who have romping in their genes.

"And then began an odyssey that made my childhood like a secret garden—with one fantastical adventure after another," says Jackie, still with a sense of wonder at the good fortune she had and how much she enjoyed it. Life in America really became a golden door for her. Alyssa's father was pleased that her new friend was a studious girl, polite, and definitely a good example of decorum. As a single father, he delighted in his daughter having a chum to share the trips, exotic dinners, and even exciting forays into the life of the city—like the time they spent playing pinball in Times Square. "Years later, it dawned on me that while I thought we had the freedom to do this one all on our own, Alyssa's dad had someone keeping tabs on us."

Jackie's parents had a comfort level with how the building staff and its residents were looking after their girls. For example, one day when the family was assembled in the elevator, Jackie's little sister introduced the astonished adults to the "nice lady" who was teaching her to sing. That was the day Jackie met the jazz legend Miss Lena Horne.

Only once does Jackie remember feeling hurt or at all resentful of the surfeit of riches that surrounded Alyssa. "I was at her mum's, and her grandparents arrived with what seemed like armfuls of beautiful clothes. There was a green velvet dress that I especially remember being so beautiful. Now I think how thoughtless it was of them to make me feel so left out. It was a lesson I never forgot."

Right after the third grade, Alyssa was sent to private school instead of attending P.S. 6. "I begged and begged everyone to reconsider, pleading my case to her parents like a barrister. Here I had come from England, made this wonderful friend, and we were to be separated. Horrors! It seemed like the end of the world. As it turned out, it didn't really affect our good times together that much. They went on for years, and they are what gave me a childhood anyone would cherish."

In addition to knowing that Alyssa was privileged in many ways, Jackie also thought she was very beautiful. Jackie especially adored what she saw as her lovely, prominent teeth. In reality, her admiration was not shared by the dentist, who installed braces just before Halloween. "I felt so terrible for A. that she wasn't able to eat the candy we collected." Those who know Jackie are not surprised that she would find an asset in what to others seemed a flaw. Acceptance is her calling card.

If Lillian Hellman had that New Year's Eve she would remember always, Jackie has an embedded memory of the cross-country camping trip she shared with Alyssa and her father, who drove the camper. "We really did camp out, but there were times when we stayed in quite grand hotels, too."

It was on that trip that Jackie got an insight into her relationship with her friend. "I had been taking a nap in the camper and woke to hear A. and her dad talking about me. I didn't really know what to do, so I decided not to interrupt them. They both agreed that what they liked about me was my happy attitude toward life. I remember feeling very warm and happy when I overheard this. It was a nice affirming moment for me."

For Jackie, what drew her to Alyssa was her unbounded generosity, a great sense of fun, adventure, and sharing, and the capacity to be a good and true friend. That they alone were the pretend girlfriends of Batman and Robin didn't hurt either. "I came to America all wide eyed, and as I look back, everything I had dreamed of came true— and much, much more, with many thanks to A. and her family."

To Each Her Own

Amy and Devin

Cornwall-on-Hudson is one of those places that gets portrayed in films and TV commercials as American as apple pie. Settled at the end of the seventeenth century, it nestles on the bank of the river, just a few miles from West Point. Because of its idyllic setting, New York City residents used to come north for the fresh air and verdant surroundings just fifty miles from the city. Amy has lived in Cornwall all her life; she recently moved into the home where her grandparents raised their children. "My family has lived in the Hudson River Valley for generations," records Amy. "From my Grandma Doris's side, the family goes back to settlers in the 1600s. I love it here. Some of us bloom where we are planted. I guess I'm just a perennial."

When Laura, Amy's younger sister, spoke at her wedding, she portrayed her "perfect" older sister as surely loving place and family, but also much, much more. It was a touching moment, because "Laura and I were never best friends growing up, even though we were close in age," Amy says of her relationship with her independent sibling, who has chosen to reside in the West. "We didn't even want to share our friends when we had someone visiting."

Everyone who knows Amy has trouble believing there are such creatures walking the earth: smart, kind, beautiful, and accomplished. But Devin was Amy's match from third grade. While Amy

Nancy Lindemeyer

was the serious student who could whip math classes like a champ, Devin was outgoing and a super athlete. Each of the friends had her own comfort zone, which wiped out any competition. "I was a shy girl who loved singing, concerts, and school plays and was always very focused on my studies. My parents met when they were both teachers, and I guess this apple didn't fall far from the tree," Amy says.

> From that first friendship, others have followed. Each enriches my life in ways that I could not have imagined. I do not have those dark, thorny, inescapable relationships called family and I miss them all the time, but I feel hugely fortunate in what I do have. . . .
> My friends go with me, take me with them, and together we bring back what we can.
>
> Margot Livesey, "The Valley of Lost Things"

"Our families were very different," she continues. "Going to Devin's house, where the rules were far more relaxed, meant getting to eat more junk food than I was allowed at home, playing card games with her large Irish Catholic family, and in the summer spending playful hours in their swimming pool."

In the fourth grade, Devin gave Amy one of those gold heart friendship necklaces that were familiar sights in grammar schools. Each wore her half as a symbol of their specialness to each other. "I was a little jealous of Devin about one thing," Amy confesses. "Her dad worked for the phone company, and the family had something like half a dozen phones in the house. We had one, and my parents used to get frustrated with how long I stayed on ours talking hour after hour to Devin. We took to sending notes to each other at school when we ended up in different classes—sometimes making lists of boys we each thought were cute. We drew even closer together during the summers when we went to our school's summer camp, first as campers and later on as counselors."

The differences in talents and goals began to draw the girls apart in high school, as Amy devoted more and more time to her honors classes and Devin became heavily involved in sports. Interestingly, however, the girls who once reveled in such activities as camp talent shows have followed similar paths. Now, at thirty, both are teachers—Amy in an elementary school, with master's degrees in science and math; Devin, not surprisingly, is a gym teacher. And they are both mothers. Amy recently had twins, Lily and Jack.

One sunny summer afternoon, she was strolling with her son and daughter tucked picture-perfect in their carriage when she encountered Devin and her mother. It was a typical scene of old friends greeting each other on one of Cornwall-on-Hudson's pretty, tree-shaded streets. They took a few minutes to chat, as neighbors are wont to do, and to adore the children before ambling on. Nothing dramatic, just taking in stride how their lives will touch, time and again, in the years ahead. Amy's husband, Tim, by the way, is one of the cute boys who made their list and, wouldn't you know, he's from a big Irish family.

Nancy Lindemeyer

An Era to Remember

Sarah and Emma

Bryn Mawr College is in the idyllic countryside just a few miles west of Philadelphia. The unusual spelling of an unusual name, meaning "large hill," comes from the Welsh language, which some wags say is "English spelled backwards." In the late nineteenth century, the founder of the college for women named the school after his Welsh home. The older residence halls resemble the spired buildings of England's Oxford University—Gothic revival structures standing like sentinels guarding the student body, which began with just thirty-six undergraduates and eight graduate scholars. Among the campus wonderments is a garden designed by Frederick Law Olmsted, and on a snowy winter's day, Pembroke Hall nestles into the white winter landscape, a romantic scene that students carry with them years after they leave academic life. One can imagine a rapturous Katharine Hepburn striding by in her days there.

When Sarah enrolled in Bryn Mawr, it was indeed a challenging time for her. While she grew up in Manhattan, she had had something of a cloistered life. "We had few visitors to our home," she recalls. "We never even had a pet to share my only-child life. Imagine my anxiety over having to sleep in the same room with another girl, and a room that was about a hundred feet square, at that. The thought of such intimacy scared me to death." Luckily, her roommate made the transition much easier for her. "Emma came from a foreign-service family and had lived all over the world. Picking up and making new friends came naturally to her, and she swept me along."

The two young women took part in all the freshman traditions together: parade and song nights and the May Day festival, which begins with students and faculty feasting on strawberries and cream. "We did so much together throughout our college years," Sarah recalls. "We ate dinner together every night and went to parties on weekends. Most upperclassmen looked to have rooms of their own; we wanted to continue to live together." There was one semester when Sarah had to live off campus by herself. "I slept through room draw," says the then "nap-addicted" Sarah. The following semester of that year, however, Emma joined her because she knew how sad Sarah was rooming alone.

Emma is remembered with tenderness for some especially kind gestures that began when Sarah was packing for her first trip home. She did not notice until opening her case back in New York the note Emma had tucked in with her clothes. "It talked about how connected she felt to me after such a short amount of time. It was then I realized I had made a real friend." Once, Emma noticed Sarah admiring a pair of earrings in a jewelry store near campus. "She got them for me, months later, as a Christmas present. I wear them to this day. A real labor of love came at the end of my senior year. I was behind in getting two papers in, both due at the same time. I typed one; Emma stayed up all night to type the other thirty-page assignment. She saved my life."

For all four years of college, Sarah and Emma were committed to keeping a record of their time together. They filled notebook after notebook with "musings and meanderings." Each recorded her impressions of things—some are serious and some are those private jokes that only the two of them could understand. When graduation came, the young women tasted the last strawberries and cream they would share together at college on the first Sunday following the end

Nancy Lindemeyer

of classes. Bryn Mawr's storybook world would soon be behind them as Sarah packed up their journals, bringing them home to New York. Emma came, too, to live for a while with Sarah's family on New York's Upper East Side.

"During the time Emma stayed with us, my mother broke her leg, and I sprained my ankle," Sarah relates. "Emma quickly became the daughter of the house, helping out with household chores like going to the supermarket and keeping our home fires burning in every way. We depended on her, as she was truly like family to us. For the first time, my parents and I let someone else into our own little world. It was such a powerful relationship for all of us, but for me especially."

Emma's next move was to California. To the consternation of Sarah and her family, they simply ceased hearing from her. "My mother and I had difficulty understanding how she could just vacate our lives the way she did." Both were deeply wounded. For Sarah, her sisterlike friend had abandoned her. Once, while Sarah was visiting California, she made an attempt to reconnect with Emma. "She gave me some vague reason why she didn't have time to get together. I was shocked. It wasn't that we'd have too many chances to see each other, living three thousand miles apart!"

But as time passed and Sarah began to reflect on the relationship, she realized that Emma's background had conditioned her to make connections and live them fully, while allowing her to move without looking back. "I just wasn't wired that way," Sarah admits. "Perhaps Emma was too easy to get to know. And as I think about all those journals we kept, resting like ancient tablets on my closet shelf untouched for years, I have to wonder why she didn't seem interested in taking half of them with her. They were as much her as me."

Sarah is now happily married, with little Madeleine in her life. Madeleine has just started preschool, and Sarah is delighted to see how her little girl, crowned with mountains of curls just like her mom's, is adjusting to the other children in her class. On a recent reunion at Bryn Mawr, Sarah discovered many changes over the years, including

Over the past year I've made contact again with the friend who had stopped speaking to me. At first, like any splintered relationship, our contact was very delicate. A passing hello at a party, a dinner where at least three other mutual friends were present. And every time I thought to myself this is too difficult, women's friendships should be easy, I realized I didn't want to stop trying because the truth was her friendship was irreplaceable.

Wendy Wasserstein, "The Ties That Wound"

how classes were being taught differently to meet the demands of new generations of students—"astonishing" to a woman who molded her college education and creative bent into a successful writing career. It was also an occasion to think about Emma.

"I've looked her up online, and I know where she lives and what she is doing. I even discovered that she, too, has a child," Sarah reveals. But she has not attempted to contact her, just as she has not been able to bring herself to delve into the Sarah-Emma notebooks. She professes, however, "I believe there will be a right time. It's not that I'm afraid. It's more like waiting for my heart to catch up with my mind." A friendship to be rekindled? Or an era to put to rest? Only time will tell which path Sarah will take.

Nancy Lindemeyer

"Heart of My Heart"

Suzy and the Keplar Street Gang

"As an only child, I have always tended to surround myself with a group of convivial friends, rather than just a single devoted one. A survey of many of us only kids I've known seems to bear this out. Some of us just liked the company of a crowd, and many learned from a very early age how to entertain themselves. And, of course, one or the other or both parents tended to be playmates and confidantes." Suzy, who has become an artist after a career as an interior designer, sends this thoughtful observation from the Mexican village where she lives now. The exotic flora has captivated her imagination, and she's been busy creating larger-than-life images with glorious colors.

"When I arrived in Mexico, I knew no one, but it was not long before I'd collected a wonderful, supportive group. That's been true wherever I've lived. I think back to the Keplar Street gang in Van Wert, Ohio, and that's where this pattern all started. Several of the kids I grew up with are still among my dearest friends, and we've been close for years. We were of a variety of ages, and some, of course, were boys, too." Suzy's parents were very different people, and both kept their separate group of friends: Her mom, Gwenelyn, was musical and artistic, and her social life centered around the church choir and the Wassenburg Art Center. Dad Harold was

wrapped up in his metal-working business and had his guy friends. "I think these role models led me to make friends around my interests," says Suzy.

Van Wert is a typical Midwestern city in lots of ways, with a few possible exceptions. In addition to the fact that it once housed the only producer of Liederkranz cheese in the world (possibly the smelliest cheese ever made), it boasts the first community library in America, the Brumbach Library. And its Victorian county courthouse is listed on the National Register of Historic Places. If one hankers for an old-fashioned Sunday chicken dinner and homemade pie, Balyeat's Coffee Shop on East Main Street is a treasure of a restaurant, run by Dale since the 1940s. (Locals love their noodles over mashed potatoes, the cafe's specialty.) Not many notables hail from this city a stone's throw from Indiana, but Suzy keeps a deep affection for her hometown, and returns now and then to exhibit her art and visit some of the old gang.

"I remember Judy and how her family, longtime residents of Keplar Street, just loved decorating the house and yard for Halloween. And this was years before giant spiders and cobwebs became a national mania," says Suzy, who thinks her friend Judy,

Nancy Lindemeyer

Little Suzy, the "Indian" at right. At left, the wee witch with the gang.

now a retired banker, is still "a kid at heart." "At one point in our young lives, when I was about six, Judy wanted to be a doctor and I, a nurse, so Mom made us darling little outfits to play in. I had this wonderful but somewhat stupid cat who allowed us to put him in a doll bed, and we'd pretend to give him medicine. Judy later turned her interests to pet snakes, and I got to share in that, too." Judy was one of the gang who came to the first opening of paintings that Suzy had at a gallery in Van Wert.

"And there's the chap that I write to on the Internet frequently. He teaches at an art college in Portland, and sometimes he thinks I'm the only person who knows where he's coming from in art and design areas. We've been friends since the first grade; maybe that's what accounts for it. Now that many of the Van Wert folk are retiring and we are seeing each other at reunions back home, it's renewed memories of our growing up. I have to smile when I think of wacky and wild tales, and now see very respectable adults standing in 'those sneakers.' By the way, it was another friend, Angie, not Judy, who actually did grow up to be a doctor—and thank goodness Angie was my chemistry lab partner in high school. That's one of the smartest things I ever did!"

Last Thanksgiving, Suzy had four invitations to dinner, American style, in the heart of Mexico. She has loyal friends she's kept from every phase of her life, and every place she has lived. She has the confidence that she knows how to make and keep friends—perhaps thanks to the Keplar Street gang and the kids of Van Wert, where neighborliness counts, in more ways than one.

Nancy Lindemeyer

HEART OF MY HEART

I sometimes wish I was a kid again
Down in the old neighborhood. . . .

"Heart of My Heart"—
   I love that melody.
"Heart of My Heart" brings back
   a memory.
When we were kids on the corner
   of the street,
We were rough and ready guys
But, oh, how we could harmonize!

"Heart of My Heart" meant friends
   were dearer then.
Too bad we had to part.
I know a tear would glisten
If once more I could listen
To the gang that sang "Heart of My Heart"

Ben Ryan, "Heart of My Heart" (1926)

Providence

"I never forgot her birthday," a grown woman says wistfully of the little girl she shared cake, ice cream, and prettily wrapped packages with. The memory remains indelible even though they have not seen each other for what seems like eons. For many there is a longing to find their way back to that favored friend. And then, by some miracle of providence, often remarkable coincidence, the quiet yearning is fulfilled amazingly bringing renewed joy and meaning to adult lives.

If one were disposed to, one might think hearts indeed have a power beyond our reason to understand. There is an old admonition about leaving nothing to chance. But here, chance proves to have some pretty powerful properties of its own.

It is not that we grow careless with our first best friends but more that we get separated for all kinds of reasons. We are young, after all, when most of this happens, and later we are distracted by a wide world opening to us. We find ourselves talking about them, sometimes to our own children. And we find ourselves searching for them in some quiet ways. Below the surface there is a desire to connect.

Providence is an inspiration for those who desire to rediscover a lost friendship. While fate can lend a hand, it can use a little help from a true desire to know again the girl you loved and discover the woman she has become.

Perhaps fate is too fickle to leave such things completely to chance—you might miss out reliving trips to the candy store, having lunch, and chatting in the understanding way old friends do. The reunion is a time to celebrate each other—and it embroiders into contemporary lives the silken threads of childhood memories.

Discovering Ourselves
Judith and Sena

W hat impels a writer to spend years uncovering the life of another? Do biographers choose their subjects, or do their subjects choose them? Judith had to learn Danish to write her award-winning biography of the writer Isak Dinesen, the Karen Blixen portrayed in the film *Out of Africa*, unlocking the essence of a fascinating life. A glance at Judith's head shot printed within her monumental work reveals a woman with dark, intense eyes, a slim nose, and a determined mouth—easily a description of Dinesen herself. And in the very first pages of the book is a small but significant paragraph that reveals a common thread in both women's lives. It has to do with their earliest friends.

For Judith, it was Sena, "an adorable girl with the cutest 'monkey legs.'" For Dinesen, it was Ellen, whom Judith reported was "a compelling figure to her friends, someone whom they were always happy to see and whom they felt honored to know." Judith, like Dinesen, saw in her friend "a simple confidence" that she could not completely have in herself.

Perhaps it was because Sena had an older sister, so her relationship with others was easier. But Judith, an only child, admired how her friend blended well with others in the topsy-turvy land of childhood. "Even as a very little girl, I felt that Sena had a mysterious understanding of life," says Judith, who readily admits that the two actually were very dissimilar. As it turned out, Judith opted for the inward life of a writer and biographer, while Sena is a social worker, dealing with the concerns of others on a daily basis.

"We really loved each other," Judith continues, "even though I was the bossy one." Sena retorts diplomatically, without missing a beat, "You never bossed me in a bad way." The two are having lunch in a tiny restaurant with cheek-by-jowl tables. "I always admired your intelligence," Sena tells Judith, "and I thought in kindergarten you would be the first woman president of the United States." Such faith in a five-year-old gave Judith an early start on confidence: "You gave me the idea I could do anything." Imagine such judgments made by little people barely more than three feet tall, although Judith was taller then and, she admits with a certain reticence, "chubby." Now she is as spare as asparagus, intense, and otherwise not much different from the way she was when the girls invented a childhood for themselves.

Both families moved to Queens, into a brand-new garden-apartment development, when the girls were about three. Queens is a borough of New York City, but it was provincial then, as Sena discovered when she went off to school at Cornell University.

"The other students expected me to be very sophisticated, being from New York City. What they didn't understand was that Queens was a world unto itself—and that world certainly wasn't very sophisticated."

"Funny that I don't remember anyone else from our early time together, although we played in the courtyard with other kids," says Judith, somewhat puzzled that her memory doesn't stretch that far back. But she and Sena cemented their relationship during those early playtimes in kindergarten at P.S. 164. After that year, the decision was made by the teacher and Sena's mother to separate the girls. Again, the issue of Judith overpowering Sena with the force of her personality came up. As the two women sit side by side now, it seems that the worry was for naught. Sena remains composed and comfortable with herself—surely not hurt a bit by Judith's early precociousness.

"I recall my mother, who was very good friends with Judith's mother, talking to her very seriously about not teaching her to read before she attended school. I don't recall what all her reasons were, but I think she thought it would look like Judith was spoiled." However, the mother who had taught English and Latin and was a great reader herself went right ahead, and Judith did begin reading at about age four. This was one indication of how different the two women were. Her eccentric, bookish mother didn't like to go outside, Judith relates, so it fell to her Aunt Charlotte to teach her how to ride a bike.

Sena's mother, on the other hand, was intent on keeping up appearances, which meant trips to the beauty parlor for hairstyling and manicures. The girls often tagged along, and it seemed like a long way for their little legs; it wasn't really, of course, being just across the courtyard. Sena's mother, the ultimate conformist, nevertheless expressed her individuality in the naming of her daughter.

"I was so impressed with Sena's name, and still am," says Judith. She asks if Sena has had to spell her name to others her whole life.

"Of course," Sena replies, "but my mother wanted me to have a name like no one else's—she about succeeded in that." On the subject of names, Judith remarks that only two people are grandfathered in to call her Judy, and Sena is one of them.

Both women reflect that neither of their families seemed particularly attuned to or interested in the playful side of their childhood. Yet playful it was. The two were in Brownies together and have fond memories of ice-skating, but the real heat in the conversation comes with the discussion of away-camp days when they were given a wonderful time-out from the routines of their family lives and became obsessed with the game of jacks. "It was insane," Judith says of the game that Sena, especially, excelled at. "I'm still pretty good," chimes in Sena. "I can see us sitting cross-legged on the floor for what

Nancy Lindemeyer

seemed like hours, engrossed in the game." An obsession for games has carried on to adult life. Both confess to being dedicated Scrabble players, including electronic Scrabble for Judith. They seem to enjoy knowing this about each other, and before the topic is exhausted, Judith says she's just now writing an article about it, sounding a little wistful that she's not still playing with Sena and hoping to rectify that in the future.

"We were mirrors of each other," says Judith, proud of the girlhood they enjoyed together. Growing up, however, meant growing apart. Each started out in adult life fulfilling the dreams she had as a child. Sena married her college sweetheart and had two children when she was quite young. Judith went to live abroad. They didn't see each other often over the years that followed. "In one of our major birthday years—I think when we were forty—we went back to Queens and walked along the streets where we grew up," Judith says, then turns to Sena: "Remember the candy store?" Well, that was the place where jacks were sold, among other games and delights like plastic lips and little bottles filled with sickeningly sweet and gooey colored liquid. That candy store just might have been the citadel of the neighborhood for them.

"Our paths diverged," says Judith, who was by far the easier to keep track of, as she wrote herself to an award-winning career and became a regular writer for *The New Yorker* magazine. It was through the magazine that Judith was given a path back to Sena, although both women declare that, if the other had ever really needed her, she would certainly have come to her aid. "One of Sena's neighbors in Larchmont [a nearby suburb] is the accountant who handles travel expenses at the magazine. This lovely woman mentioned Sena to me, and it wasn't long before we were having lunch together and rediscovering ourselves—each of us is the repository of so many memories of the other. It is moving for me to hear what she has to say, and remembers."

Sena leaves the restaurant bound for the airport to pick up her son. Judith is on deadline for a story and has some son obligations of her own, with Will being home from college for the summer. But before they bustle off, Judith suggests, with a sense of occasion, that they plan to celebrate the anniversary of their meeting—a big year is not far off. "Birthdays were so important to us, and no matter where I was in the world, I always thought of Sena on her birthday, but our anniversary is an event the two of us can share equally." The adorable thin little girl and the one who thought she was awkward and chubby, who hung over the candy store counter together picking out games and treats, who shared camp tales and envied each other's lives in one way or another ("Sena got to share her bedroom with a sister; I would have liked that") are marking their calendars for a momentous time together, thanks to a neighbor and coworker who one day played the role of an angel of providence.

Nancy Lindemeyer

"Scrappy Little Girls"
Carolyn and Cynthia

It always amazed Walter Farley, the author of the Black Stallion books, that most of his mail was from girls. Bemused, he said that he didn't think boys liked animals less but that girls wrote more letters. Farley's mail went on for forty years as one book after another was written, twenty-one in all, and grabbed up by new generations who became devotees of the action, excitement, and suspense the books provided.

In the first book, the classic written when Farley was in high school, the other characters can't fathom the relationship between Alex, the young hero, and his horse: "The friendship between the boy and the stallion was something too much for them to understand." Perhaps the girls from the age of seven or eight who loved the stories so much identified with that mysterious bond—just ask Carolyn and Cynthia.

"We read seven of them together," recalls Carolyn, who admits to a shorter attention span. Cindy, her girlhood name, remembers devouring all there were at the time. One day, coming home from school, the two began to run as fast as they could. It was a horse race to the finish line. And Carolyn—who describes the two as "scrappy little girls, never afraid of anything"—won. Why, neither can understand now, but they didn't speak after that for several weeks.

This, however, wasn't normal for the girls, who virtually lived in

Cynthia (left) and Carolyn are leaders at the Fourth of July parade.

the same house in the Shaker Heights neighborhood of Cleveland, Ohio. It was not a typical duplex but a big structure on a corner, so that each family had its own porch and entrance. When one of the girls wanted to signal the other to come out and play, they devised a whistling sound that was theirs alone. "If Carolyn didn't come out right away, I'd just sit on the back steps and wait for her, no matter how long it took, and it used to worry my mother that I was too attached. I suspect that I knew the fun wouldn't start without her high energy and intense personality. And maybe because we were never in the same class at school, our time together had its own specialness."

Dear Judge Hoover next door, a bit like the kindly but often perturbed neighbor in *Dennis the Menace*, seemed to be annoyed when the two climbed his tree and jumped onto his well-manicured lawn. Every Saturday, he would find them in his kitchen in one of their calmer moments. Mrs. Hoover became a real presence in their lives. "Remember Madge, the manicurist on TV," Carolyn asks, "the one who used to soak her customers' fingertips in a solution of water and Palmolive soap to soften their cuticles? Well, Mrs. Hoover, probably trying to civilize us, used to give us manicures just like that. I still make the sugar cookies with the Red Hots in the center that she used to bake for us, and my boys love them just the way

Nancy Lindemeyer

Cindy and I used to—with a glass of cold milk. Her own grandchildren lived far away, and I think we were her fill-in grandkids."

Carolyn moved to Colorado when she was thirteen, and Cindy feels she has never had a friend like her since. "I continued to go to the Hoovers' on Saturday, spending time with Mrs. Hoover, just like we both had done. On Sunday, after church, it became a ritual for me to recite, as closely as I could remember, the minister's sermon to the judge. Once, when we were sitting outside, he looked at me with a glint in his eye and asked if I didn't want to shinny up his tree. I think he knew how much I missed Carolyn."

Their mothers, who had become good friends, too, continued to keep in touch (Cindy's parents still live in the same house), but the childhood friends from Fourth of July parades, puppet shows, forbidden short-cuts through neighbors' yards, diving into snow piles, and the Elvis Presley marathon playing the same record thirty-three times in a row—weren't as diligent. Their adult lives accelerated, with both marrying young and having two sons—virtually on the same timetable. Cindy is married to an Anglican priest and lives in Texas. Carolyn married Gerard, a restaurateur in New York, and became a pastry chef and food stylist, working for a time for Martha Stewart's television program.

Shortly after Carolyn left the show, her mom told her that Cindy's son was scheduled to appear on it. John-Paul, at thirteen, was becoming famous for his uncanny ability to invest successfully in the stock market. After a flurry of phone calls, the event was the occasion for a reunion dinner at Carolyn and Gerard's restaurant. "I was in jeans," Carolyn says, "and we both had to laugh, because I was allowed to wear jeans when we were little kids and Cindy wasn't. She always hated that!"

When Cindy, who some time ago grew into the name of Cynthia, reflects on her friend, it seems that Walter Farley's words definitely apply—only the two of them truly understand "the combination of us," as Cynthia expresses it. "Carolyn helped me become who I am."

And part of that was accepting challenge and adventure. Recently, Cynthia emailed photographs to Carolyn of her mission to Peru, where she was involved in bringing eyeglasses to people in poor villages.

Carolyn, in the characteristically relaxed way that Cynthia has always admired, appreciates her friend's steadfastness and thinks of the time at the pool one summer when they both did backflips off the ten-foot diving board all afternoon long. Yep, in Carolyn's plain talk, they were "scrappy little kids."

Nancy Lindemeyer

MRS. HOOVER'S RED HOTS SUGAR COOKIES

Makes approximately 60 cookies

1 pound butter, at room temperature
3 cups granulated sugar
2 eggs
1½ teaspoons salt
1½ teaspoons vanilla extract
5 cups all-purpose flour
Sparkling sugar (bright white) to coat
1 box Red Hots candy

Using an electric mixer with a paddle attachment, beat the butter and sugar on medium-high until light and fluffy (5 to 7 minutes). Add the eggs one at a time and mix until incorporated. Add the salt and vanilla. With the mixer on low speed, add the flour and mix until just combined.

Divide the dough in half. To make a 3" round cookie, roll each half into a log approximately 2" in diameter and wrap with parchment paper. Chill until firm.

Preheat the oven to 350°F. Roll the log in sparkling bright white sugar and slice it into quarter-inch-thick rounds. On a cookie sheet lined with parchment paper, place the rounds about 1 inch apart all around. Place one Red Hots candy in the center of each slice. Bake for 12 to 15 minutes, until slightly golden around the edges (do not overbake).

Cool completely on a wire rack.

You Are What You Wear

Shirtspantskirtsdresseshoesockscoatsweaters.

Layer upon layer

of clothes,

all codified

and chosen

with precision.

What you wore determined your day,

and a day could feel like a lifetime

when you were eight.

Dressing was destiny.

One seriously wrong move

and you were vulnerable,

or a victim,

and even before you had hips

you had hipsters to contend with.

But through it all

you had your girlfriend,

whose style

and silhouette

you knew as well as your own.

You could have picked out her wardrobe

in a dark room

wearing sunglasses.

Her fashion philosophy?

Preppy.

Girlie girl.

Or suffering under the tyranny of matchy-matchy,

you envied/admired/frowned upon her choices.

You found your wardrobe

in a mirror.

You found your style

in relation to hers.

—Robin Reiser

Moments of Perception
Janet and Elsie

On a late September afternoon, the bright yellow taxicabs rushing by seem almost like fall leaves in flight along the crowded, cozy streets of New York's Greenwich Village. The sky is azure, like the blue chalk in an artist's box, with streaks of white from jets streaming over the city. It's the day that Janet and Elsie make their seasonal visit to the Eskandar shop on 10th Street. The space is gallerylike, clean and well lit, and the clothes, made of natural fabrics, in exquisite colors, hang unadorned in dramatic shapes—this season, a cranberry color stands out. These two women enjoy shopping together, stopping for tea in one of the little restaurants, and often going to the Metropolitan Museum of Art, the Modern, the Morgan Library, or any of several outstanding galleries.

September reminds the two friends of their initial meeting—in line to register for art school in Philadelphia many, many years ago. "We just started chatting," says Janet, "and we were best friends throughout our four years of art school." One of the things they enjoyed at the time, and still recall with delight, is seeing the film star Ava Gardner at Saks Fifth Avenue when they were on a school trip to New York. "She was absolutely exquisite—a work of art herself," recalls Janet, still amazed by their good fortune.

Both Elsie and Janet came to New York when they graduated, remaining close and continuing to take art classes. Elsie excelled at

Nancy Lindemeyer

illustration for children's books, and Janet worked in advertising, in one assignment using her incredible needlework skills for a "Home Sweet Home" sampler used in a campaign. She also had a long association with a cosmetic company to do fantastical package design and worked for craft magazines creating stitchery projects.

All the while, Janet continued to attend classes for inspiration and to improve her skills, but no longer with Elsie, who had moved to New Jersey. They simply drifted apart in the vast population of the New York art scene. Both were married, and new lives took them in different directions.

Janet's favorite teacher and mentor, Jack, became a trusted friend along the gathering years over their easels. About fifteen years ago, Jack approached Janet with a suggestion. There was a woman in one of his classes who was not only intelligent but progressing nicely with her studies, and he talked about how she was mastering shapes and achieving beautiful compositions. "Janet," he said, "I think you should meet her; she is so much like you, I know you will hit it off." Janet was amused and touched. Indeed, the woman sounded like an ideal match, and when Jack began to describe her, Janet had a weird sense of recognition. The more Jack talked about the woman in his class, the more she began to think he just might be talking about her old friend, Elsie.

"'I think I know her. Does her name begin with an *E*?' I asked him," Janet recalls. After a few more probing questions in what turned out to be a sort of cat-and-mouse game, Janet confessed that she knew he was describing Elsie. "How could you know that?" Jack insisted, a bit discouraged that his find was a rediscovery rather than a revelation. But through him, Janet was reunited with an old and treasured friend, and the two again walked in concert in the same ways they had when their hair was shoulder length and they wore matching pleated skirts and black tights so that one could hardly tell them apart. Interestingly, many years before, Janet had been the one who had recommended Jack as a teacher to Elsie.

Elsie and Janet began attending Jack's classes together, both searching to develop skills and explore new mediums. Since his death a few years ago, both women miss his incredible talents as a teacher and his insights, not only into art but into the art of living as well. They are both grateful, too, for his acuity as a matchmaker. However, the coveted classes with one of Jack's former students continue happily. And they have continued their frequent phone calls and appointments for the activities they enjoy most—exhibitions and art shows.

> *What is one's personality, detached from that of the friends with whom fate happens to have linked one.*
>
> Edith Wharton, *A Backward Glance*

"Elsie is so very grounded," says Janet, "as well as being practical and wise. After all these years, our friendship just gets better and better. It has just been a gift, I like to think, from our dear Jack." When asked about the most meaningful show that she and Elsie attended together in recent years, Janet moves forward in her chair and fingers her teacup as she pauses to reflect on the many times they have paused in front of paintings, with the reverence that students have for masters, carefully taking in all the magnificent details.

"I would have to say the Museum of Modern Art's retrospective on the French Impressionist Pierre Bonnard," Janet responds, as a knowing expression crosses her face and her eyes, as blue as the table covering in Bonnard's *Dining Room in the Country*, light up.

Nancy Lindemeyer

One of the reviews of this show referred to Bonnard's "extremely discrete moments of perception"—and obviously two mature women who have spent their lives in pursuit of excellence in art would be attentive to such an achievement. Bonnard's paintings offer them a parallel universe to dwell in. As women, they are captivated by the elegant everyday quality of his work, say, in a painting like *Dressing Table and Mirror*. As artists, they can contemplate the highest levels of composition and technique. As Janet and Elsie study *Regatta*, with its montage of women's hats in the foreground and intense colors, Bonnard draws them to the profile of an innocent-looking boy who is the soul of the painting—the human touch that transcends the commonplace. How often one wants to turn to someone with an observation or comment, only to be silenced by the thought that it would take too much time to describe one's feelings and that the effort would be wasted. How reassuring, then, to have a friend who can, even without speaking, know your heart and mind.

Whether or not there are bags in their arms as they leave Eskandar, they will have reveled in the artistry of the clothes, evaluated the new colors in the line, and made a date to check in again soon. It's just down the street from the loft Janet shares with her artist husband—a familiar environment for Elsie. This is a friendship begun in the study of art and thriving in that lifelong passion, along with a healthy helping of quiet respect for talent and tenderness. And, perhaps like a Bonnard painting, an understanding and appreciation of intimacy.

Bundles of Security
Claire and Lynn

"What we have in common is that neighborhood that still holds a place in my dreams: no fences, scrawny trees, sidewalks and bikes and kids wandering freely, each split-level like the next, going to see old Mrs. Cohen around the corner, learning to thread a needle and tie a knot with Mrs. Lipwitch, day-old bagels from Sol next door, drinking out of Flintstone jelly glasses at Randi and Cindy's house, sleeping over, walking to school, dressing up our bikes for the parades in the park across the street—a place I walk in happiness." So writes Claire, an accomplished author.

The girls, Claire and Lynn, were about eight or nine when they collaborated on one of Claire's first imaginative works, "The Polka-Dotted Kangaroo," which unfortunately has been lost. Claire wrote the story, and Lynn provided the illustrations. Claire went on to write several books with her dad and become an editor and writer on her own. Lynn, the youthful illustrator, made a career in art as a therapist and teacher. "Claire always wanted to be a writer like her mom and dad," Lynn recalls, as the women relax with their families during an old-friends reunion at the Jersey shore. Claire's kids are flirting with the ocean waves as Lynn's older daughter keeps an eye on them.

A tide of all the shared elements of their lives comes flooding back on this rare visit. The women were born just days apart in the

Best dresses and best behavior—Claire (left) and Lynn.

same hospital, but it was not until they were three and their families both moved to a new development that the closeness began. The people living in the development were mostly Jewish, and Claire recalls that Lynn's family was rollicking and lively in contrast to her more restrained and studious home environment. "Claire is the only Unitarian I've ever met," says Lynn, who enjoyed being included in the Christmas morning festivities at Claire's, when she was called to collect the present Santa left for her under the tree.

"Claire's mother, Helen, was always composed, almost ethereal, but when Claire and I tossed a blanket over her dining-room table one time to make a fort and held down the corners with some precious books, she was not impressed with our creativity and told my mother that we were roughhousing," Lynn reports, still with a sheepishness about the embarrassing incident.

Claire describes her home as always having "a sense of quiet"— "I see my father tall, my mother happy, wearing her classic shirt-waists, a book coming out, Aunt Vera close by." Helen's wardrobe intrigued Lynn's mother because it was so unvarying and fitted her pencil-thin frame to perfection. Forever after, she called the style "Helen dresses."

Carrie, Claire's youngest, walks across the room. Lynn smiles at her grace and can't help but compare her steps to her mother's walk as a child. "My mother used to so admire this about Claire, her silent stride." The girls were inseparable from three to seven, and then Lynn's family moved, but there were still times when they got together at each other's home, until they were about eleven. Those magical years have left lasting and enriching impressions. "I wanted to name my daughter Claire, but with our last name it didn't have the same flow," Lynn says. As for Claire, her writing abounds with characters named Lynn. "I don't think I've had that kind of friendship since Lynn and I parted—the kind where someone is always there for you, ready to be a party to an adventure, to invent a world, play Barbies, and be arm in arm day after day. Lynn was my saddle-shoed bundle of security. I've always been drawn to women named Lynn— and now the original is back."

It seems more than fate, the story of how these two women reunited. Lynn just happened to notice the masthead of a magazine where Claire was listed as a contributing editor. "I almost didn't write her," Lynn admits. "It took me about six months to decide to do it, because it had been so long, and I didn't know how she would respond." Publishing offices being what they are, it took another half a year for Claire to receive the letter, but it thrilled her. "I could hardly believe that Lynn's son was going to college in the town where I live, and it was not long before we were having happy times again, now including our families." Celebrating Lynn's son's graduation was such a special event. "It just amazes me how harmonious we all are," says Claire. "Hey, I married a Jewish guy! Maybe being around Lynn's family as a kid had something to do with it."

On this day by the ocean, the women enjoy the comings and goings typical of the casual lifestyle of a summer beach house and talk about family and life events. Lynn's brother, a children's book illustrator, and his wife have blended into the mix of grown-ups, a fresh-faced teenager, and that graceful nine-year-old.

Marriages? Claire took some time to decide on a thoughtful art director and book designer. "He was unusually kind to a fellow

Nancy Lindemeyer

writer—and I admired that so much because art directors can be difficult to deal with." As for Lynn, she knew the minute she laid eyes on the hospital supervisor at her first job. "I announced I was going to marry him; but a coworker pointed out that there was a slight problem—because he was so shy, he wouldn't even speak to me at the time."

And what about Claire's dad? "I have been so proud to have my name linked to his on our books, and in his eighties, he is still researching and planning new ones. *Real Life at the White House* is one of my favorites, because it reveals the intimate details of first families—squabbles, pets, china patterns—the things left out of ordinary histories. And I was so fortunate once to spend several days with Lady Bird Johnson at her ranch in Texas for a magazine assignment. We had lunch and held hands in prayer around her table. That was a real-life experience for me, that's for sure."

For a few moments, these two accomplished women are little girls again, sitting at a table in Helen's kitchen drawing pictures and writing a story together while Helen makes grilled-cheese sandwiches ("the cheese was Velveeta, but the bread wholesome") and promises the coveted fizzy drinks—"if we were good." When the girls got older, Helen, hoping to secure some peace at her typewriter, would dub her kitchen a place of "helpie selfie."

"This is a world I have tried to create ever since," Claire says wistfully. "Connection and rootedness without too many restraints— but on a grown-up level, with dinners and kids flowing pretty much unfettered. Hopeful. Inspirational. Surrounded by the evidence of time, the place where love comes from."

As for Lynn and all she meant to Claire once, "She's back for good." They'll see each other in the Amish Country of Pennsylvania in the fall. Something new and welcome is happening in lives that touched so fleetingly once upon a time.

A Miracle in Brooklyn
Larisa and Irina

"**M**y very favorite gift from Irina, when we were children, was a little bottle of perfume," says Larisa, now a thirty-year-old mother of two. "It was a quite tiny bottle, the kind that has a stopper instead of a cap. Somehow the stopper came loose, and before I realized it, all the perfume had leaked out. I was especially sad because every time I had worn that scent, I felt Irina's presence very close to me. It could not be replaced, so I only had the sweet memory of it then, and I still remember how it made me feel. Irina loves giving parties and gifts for any occasion, especially for our birthdays each November and December. She's a wonderful compliment to me, my other side, as she is the outgoing one."

Larisa and Irina both came to America from Uzbekistan—from the ancient city of Bukhara—when they were nine and eight, respectively. How different their new homes in New York City, must have seemed to them. Their native country was centuries old and at one time famous for being on the Silk Road from Europe to China. Marco Polo, the Italian explorer, traveled this storied route, as did generations of traders to exotic lands. Their country also saw thousands of years of wars, conquests, and religious strife.

Their city, reported to be founded in the thirteenth century BC, has a rich heritage representing the many cultures that influenced life there over the centuries. Larisa and Irina were born into

Nancy Lindemeyer

a country that was then part of the Soviet Union, and while their language was Russian, their Orthodox Jewish faith was not always welcome within the region. A significant number of Jews chose to leave Bukhara, even after Soviet rule ended in 1991. Thousands came to America and settled in cities such as New York.

Once it was the simple and pure gift of a scent that expressed the close attachment of these two young girls. But for many years now, their friendship has been the harmony of their everyday lives. Throughout most of their school years they studied side by side, including college. Both trained to be opticians—a profession that has allowed them to work part-time while raising their families. Larisa has a son, Jonathan, who is eight, and a daughter, Adelina, sixteen months old. Irina is the mother of a six-month-old daughter, Kyla, and a toddler, Maria. The women have arranged their schedules so that they are able to help each other out and raise their children together. "We hoped to be pregnant for Adelina and Maria at the same time. And indeed we were pretty close," Larisa says. "Hopefully the girls will grow up as inseparable as we are," she says with a touch of prayer in her soft voice, which still carries a slight accent.

Their closeness was fostered at a yeshiva for girls in Brooklyn. Be'er Hagolah was founded in 1979 with the mission to help Jewish children who were immigrating from the Soviet Union. There was a need for these children to learn how to become Americans without losing their own beautiful heritage. Looking after the well-being of the girls included nurturing their hearts as well as their minds. When Larisa relates how she met her first best friend at this school, a story begins that is worthy of the term "miracle."

"Irina and I came to America each with one parent: I with my father and she with her mother." Larisa says. "At school, we girls who were enrolling for the first time were given evaluations as to what level, rather than class, we would be assigned to." On the first day of school all the students were clad in uniforms; "We all looked alike,"

Larisa recalls. It was on this September day that their lives were forever changed. Larisa remembers sitting in the classroom waiting patiently for the teacher to call her name when she heard her last name paired with the first name "Irina" instead of her own. "I was stunned," Larisa says, "and it was then that I realized I had found the sister I was separated from at the age of five."

The girls' parents had divorced, and under rare circumstances, one child went with each parent. Larisa was in their father's care, as she was the oldest. The separation so grieved her that for the next four years she never stopped peering at the faces of little girls who looked Irina's age, especially the ones with curly hair, hoping to find her little sister. "We both had curly hair then, but now we work very hard to have straight hair," she says, touching one of her dark locks and rolling her eyes.

"When the astonished teachers realized the situation, they shared in our excitement. We were taken to the principal's office, and our mother was called. On that one day, I found my sister, my first best friend for life, and my mother," Larisa says, still with a sense of awe.

How quickly life changed for the sisters, and what joy has transpired over the years that followed. At first, the differences between the parents had to be bridged, and that was not always easy. But with time, the love the girls had for each other—and the lengths they went to be together—formed a healing bond. Because they were so devoted to each other, Larisa and Irina missed out on the squabbles that school friends often engage in. "We had a group of friends, but none were as important to us as we were to each other," Larisa recounts.

"If it were not for my sister looking out for me," Larisa relates with a smile in her intensely brown eyes, "I would not have found my husband." Irina was engaged and her fiancé's friend Rafael seemed to have just the qualities Larisa wanted in a husband. The only problem was that this young man was already attached. Irina didn't give up, though, and kept an eye on the development of that

Nancy Lindemeyer

relationship. When it ended, Irina was the matchmaker—who made a very good match. Three months later, Larisa married Rafael, with her sister at her side. "I knew the minute I saw him, I would marry him," Larisa says.

"Having my sister as my best friend has been the most wonderful thing in my life. From that first day at school, we have had the joy of building a family again. Our parents are loving grandparents to our four children, and so happy that life has brought us all together again. I always tell my children, 'You would not be here except for Aunt Irina.'"

There is a song from a classic Broadway musical about a hundred million miracles happening every day. Larisa and Irina are one of them, a miracle in an unlikely place like Brooklyn, a million miles from heartbreak and Bukhara, Uzbekistan. "We lost four years of our lives together, but we have made up for it in so many, many ways," Larisa affirms. Both women now make their homes in Queens, as do many of their friends and family members from Bukhara. They are all Americans, having traveled the road from East to West, bringing with them old traditions and creating new ones.

I call my sister and hear water running
three thousand miles away.
"What're you washing?"
"A sweater. You?"
"Laying one out to dry."

Susan Minot, "Forever Entwined"

Afterword

Jan and her daughter shopped my legs tired on a visit last spring. When we stopped for lunch or tea, all three of us lingered longer than usual over salads and cups. These were more than rest stops. They were times for Jan and Sue to catch me up on all the doings of their large and close family. There were sweet moments to talk about Jan's brother, Robert, who died recently. Robert came home from the Navy when Jan's mother died to help their dad with raising her. He was a good steward of my girlhood, too. Uncle Robert was beloved by Jan's kids for all the same reasons.

I adored watching the little-girl delight Jan felt as she posed with the snappy doormen at the Plaza Hotel—shades of the precocious Eloise in a giddy grandmother, it seemed to me. Her super-winning smile wrapped the chaps in gold braid around her little finger. And she and Sue had as much fun bargaining with the street sellers as they did singing with the clerks in a SoHo shop. Seattle hit New York with a lot of West Coast energy and enthusiasm.

For us—the pride of Lincoln School and the darlings of teachers like wise and warm Mrs. Graham—restoring a friendship has given a sweet new dimension to our lives. When February 28 rolls around, I no longer wonder whatever happened to Janice Foster. I know that Jan Barth is just moving into a new home. She tore down her old house and—with the support of her five kids, their burgeoning

Nancy Lindemeyer

families, and a contractor with the patience of Job—built her dream house. I know that she's chosen blue and white for her kitchen color scheme. Blue and white! I've always loved that combination, too. On my too-close-to-Christmas birthday, I can look forward to a call from Jan and the girls in the family. She's told them about having one of my grandmother's mile-high cakes at our big round oak table in the huge old kitchen where we shared a family meal. The windows would be frosted over, and holiday spirits were high.

While many things have changed—Jan adds a dash of onion powder to her dad's egg salad sandwich recipe—many others have not. She's still a charmer, and I'm still a worrier.

I've never had a single close intimate girl-friend in all my life. I never had a chum to whom I could confide my secrets. I suppose that accounts for the fact that now it is so painfully difficult for me to open my heart and confide in people who are, so often, almost strangers. You have to learn so very young to open your heart.

Jean Arthur, film star of the 1930s and 1940s

Acknowledgments

We have remembered together, laughed together, and shared bittersweet times. The dozens of women whose memories are told in this book—I thank them, especially, for allowing me into their private worlds. They are, in alphabetical order: Bernadette Baczynski, Virginia Clausen Behrens, Tracey Bishkin, Shannon Boehm, Katie Bruxvoort, Ann L. Burckhardt, Lynn Cashell, Carol Cody, Crystal Cohagan, Jennifer DeLuca, Nancy Kraut DeSimone, Jacqueline Deval, Vera Elezovic, Tricia Foley, Mary Forsell, Kathleen Foster, Lynn Shay Harrod, Kat Hendrix, Phoebe Hunter, Dr. Suzanne Ildstad, Tammy Jacob, Judy Jones, Mary Kennedy, Anna Lenz, Ann Levine, Connie Livsey, Susan Maher, Celeste Iberti Marcus, Kath Maxwell, Janet McCaffery, Mary Miller Moss, Larisa Mirakova, Karen Noske, Cynthia Pigeon, Carolyn Renny, Amy Kuhar Reynolds, Bethany Saint Smith, Retta Sassower, Wendi Schneider, Debbie Segal, JoAnn Summey, Suzy Taylor, Judith Thurman, Pat Kerr Tigrett, Melanie Frazier Tragesser, Sena Warner, Claire Whitcomb, Carol Zempel.

Cynthia Cohan and Virginia Otis generously contributed stories, photographs, and poems about their mother, Par, and her friend Betsy; Peter Kiernan also kindly remembered his mother, Betsy, and Par. Kitty Ball Ross, their family friend, brought this heartwarming story to my attention.

Nancy Lindemeyer

Ciba Vaughan and Jackie Deval were early cheerleaders that *My First Best Friend* become a book. Making that happen with grace and charm were Leslie Stoker, the publisher of Stewart, Tabori & Chang; my editor, Kristen Latta; and Lana Lê of woolypear—all old souls. Ann Stratton cheerfully shepherded final details.

When I asked Robin Reiser, a friend and former colleague, to write a series of tone poems about girlhood "stuff"—she responded gleefully with her usual knack of saying things that bring flashes of recognition and humor in a very few lines. I am proud to have her original poems in this book.

Mary Forsell's literary taste is far reaching and exquisite, and I thank her for bringing the voices and wisdom of female writers to the book.

Denise Di Novi has been gracious in taking time from a busy film career to write a foreword with a wonderful story of her own.

The folks at Lindemeyer Productions—Barbara Lynn Cantone and Daniel D'Arrezzo—were invaluable to me. In doing so many tasks, they allowed me to concentrate on the heart and soul of these stories. Robert Lindemeyer, husband and partner in life and business, remembered well and read even better. Paul Lindemeyer, son and partner, brought technical skills and the pleasure of his company. And Kitty Foyle, devoted pet, kept things peaceful and calm from her perch in the solarium next to my desk.

Published in 2010 by Stewart, Tabori & Chang
An imprint of ABRAMS

Copyright © 2010 by Lindemeyer Productions, Inc.

Library of Congress Cataloging-in-Publication Data:

Lindemeyer, Nancy.
    My first best friend : thirty stories, lifetime memories / by Nancy Lindemeyer.
p. cm.
ISBN 978-1-58479-835-4 (alk. paper)
1. Best friends. 2. Friendship in children. 3. Female friendship. I. Title.
BF575.F66L57 2010
155.9'25—dc22   2009002290

Editor: Kristen Latta
Designer: woolypear
Production Manager: Tina Cameron

The text of this book was composed in Avenir, Bodoni Egyptian, and School Script.

Stewart, Tabori & Chang books are available at special discounts when purchased in quantity
for premiums and promotions as well as fundraising or educational use. Special editions can
also be created to specification. For details, contact specialmarkets@abramsbooks.com or
the address below.

Printed and bound in the United States.
10 9 8 7 6 5 4 3 2 1

115 West 18th Street
New York, NY 10011
www.abramsbooks.com